# THE LAST
# CHEROKEE
# WARRIORS

# THE LAST CHEROKEE WARRIORS

Zeke Proctor       Ned Christie

## PHILLIP STEELE

PELICAN PUBLISHING COMPANY
GRETNA 1987

First edition, April 1974
Second edition, January 1987


Library of Congress Cataloging-in-Publication Data

Steele, Phillip W.
    The last Cherokee warriors.

    Bibliography: p.
    1. Proctor, Ezekiel, 1831-1907. 2. Christie, Ned,
1852-1892. 3. Cherokee Indians—Biography. 4. Cherokee
Indians—History. 5. Indians of North America—Okla-
homa—History. 6. Indians of North America—Arkansas—
History. I. Title.
E99.C5P837      1987      976.6'00497      86-25348
ISBN: 0-88289-643-1


Manufactured in the United States of America

Published by Pelican Publishing Company, Inc.
1101 Monroe Street, Gretna, Louisiana 70053

Designed by Oscar Richard

To MEAGAN and JASON

With the hope that this work
will inspire them to share
their father's keen interest in
America's frontier history.

# CONTENTS

PREFACE     9

**PART ONE: EZEKIEL PROCTOR**

I     The Proctor Family     15

II     The Man and His Lawless Environment     22

III     Zeke and His Family     30

IV     The Beck Mill Incident     34

V     The Trial     40

VI     Amnesty and Zeke's Treaty
with the United States     48

VII     Best-Known Proctor Fables     61

**PART TWO: NED CHRISTIE**

VIII     The Man and His Bitterness     69

IX     The Murder of Deputy Marshal Maples     79

X     Christie's Four Long Years of War     87

XI     The Final Siege     94

BIBLIOGRAPHY     109

# Cherokee Alphabet.

| | | | | | |
|---|---|---|---|---|---|
| Ꭰ a | Ꭱ e | Ꭲ i | Ꭳ o | Ꭴ u | Ꭵ v |
| Ꭶ ga Ꭷ ka | Ꭸ ge | Ꭹ gi | Ꭺ go | Ꭻ gu | Ꭼ gv |
| Ꭽ ha | Ꭾ he | Ꭿ hi | Ꮀ ho | Ꮁ hu | Ꮂ hv |
| Ꮃ la | Ꮄ le | Ꮅ li | Ꮆ lo | Ꮇ lu | Ꮈ lv |
| Ꮉ ma | Ꮊ me | Ꮋ mi | Ꮌ mo | Ꮍ mu | |
| Ꮎ na Ꮏ hna Ꮐ nah | Ꮑ ne | Ꮒ ni | Ꮓ no | Ꮔ nu | Ꮕ nv |
| Ꮖ qua | Ꮗ que | Ꮘ qui | Ꮙ quo | Ꮚ quu | Ꮛ quv |
| Ꮜ sa Ꮝ s | Ꮞ se | Ꮟ si | Ꮠ so | Ꮡ su | Ꮢ sv |
| Ꮣ da Ꮤ ta | Ꮥ de Ꮦ te | Ꮧ di Ꮨ ti | Ꮩ do | Ꮪ du | Ꮫ dv |
| Ꮬ dla Ꮭ tla | Ꮮ tle | Ꮯ tli | Ꮰ tlo | Ꮱ tlu | Ꮲ tlv |
| Ꮳ tsa | Ꮴ tse | Ꮵ tsi | Ꮶ tso | Ꮷ tsu | Ꮸ tsv |
| Ꮹ wa | Ꮺ we | Ꮻ wi | Ꮼ wo | Ꮽ wu | Ꮾ wv |
| Ꮿ ya | Ᏸ ye | Ᏹ yi | Ᏺ yo | Ᏻ yu | Ᏼ yv |

## Sounds Represented by Vowels

a, as a in father, or short as a in rival

e, as a in hate, or short as e in met

i, as i in pique, or short as i in pit

o, as o in note, approaching aw in law

u, as oo in fool, or short as u in pull

v, as u in but, nasalized

## Consonant Sounds

g nearly as in English, but approaching to k. d nearly as in English but approaching to t. h k l m n q s t w y as in English. Syllables beginning with g except Ꭶ (ga) have sometimes the power of k. Ꭺ (go), Ꮪ (du), Ꮫ (dv) are sometimes sounded to, tu, tv and syllables written with tl except Ꮭ (tla) sometimes vary to dl.

# PREFACE

As the American frontier moved westward, Indians found it necessary to fight with whatever means they had to preserve the lands their tribes had occupied for hundreds of years. Treated as wild and insensitive savages who had no right to these lands, one by one the tribes encountered the white man and either were slaughtered in battle or forcibly moved farther west. There was little communication between the white man and the Indian, other than arrow or bullet, because neither could fully understand the language or point of view of the other. Among Indians, only the Cherokees had an alphabet, and, being somewhat better educated and advanced, they realized the hopelessness of waging war against insurmountable odds. Rather than go to war, they chose to negotiate peaceably with the white man, and for doing so, they were severely criticized by such warring tribes as the Apache and Sioux. These negotiations to keep their rich farmlands and homes in the Carolinas and Georgia failed, however, and they were forced to accept a treaty that would move their nation to the region that is now eastern Oklahoma.

Thousands of deaths resulted from extreme hardships during the great Indian removal, known historically as the Trail of Tears. Forced removal from their lands left a great bitterness in the hearts of the Cherokees, but, realizing there was no recourse, they settled their new lands peaceably and began working to rebuild their nation on territory they could now call their own. Their treaties with the United States assured them the right to develop their own government, the right of property ownership, and the right to establish their own laws and judicial system.

As the American frontier pushed westward, however, the Cherokees soon found the United States again interfering with their judicial system; and whites were settling lands within the new Indian nation. These actions were considered by the Cherokees to be in violation of their original treaties, and the bitterness toward the United States grew to a stage of near war.

Through an unusual set of circumstances a half-breed Cherokee named Ezekiel Proctor became the tribe's leader in its last revolt against United States interference in the Cherokee judicial system. During Proctor's subsequent trial eleven men lost their lives, and during the months that followed, scores of United States marshals and white citizens along the Arkansas and Indian nation border were killed. United States authorities held Zeke Proctor and his band of followers responsible for these deaths, but fearing that Proctor's prosecution would cause a major Indian uprising, President U. S. Grant found it necessary to issue a treaty or amnesty with him. In the United States government's only treaty with an individual, peace was restored, and, temporarily at least, the tense situation was resolved.

The Keetoowa Society, an Indian religious order, had supported Zeke Proctor's rebellion against United States authority within the Cherokee system of government. Watt Christie and his son Ned were Keetoowa leaders. They and other members realized that Proctor's treaty had saved Proctor and many of his supporters from hanging, but it had not solved the problem of federal intervention within their nation. Ned Christie and many of the Cherokee patriots considered the treaty to be a surrender.

As the railroads were built and increasing numbers of white traders and merchants came into the Cherokee nation, white citizens began settling on Cherokee lands under the protection of the many United States marshals who rode out of Judge Isaac Parker's federal court in Fort Smith, Arkansas. While this apparent infraction of the Cherokee right of landownership grew more prominent, Ned Christie's bitterness turned to rage. Soon finding himself surrounded by circumstances similar to those that faced Proctor, he gathered a small band of followers and once more struck out against the invaders. After four years of battle with the marshals, Christie was killed in a volley of thirty-eight rounds from a cannon.

Some observers consider Proctor and Christie to have been nothing more than outlaws, but by most Cherokees they are remembered as the last of their tribe to stand up for their lands against the encroachment that resulted in the eventual loss of a proud nation. It is not the purpose of this book to establish Zeke Proctor and Ned Christie as outlaws or martyrs, but rather to examine the lives of two belligerent Cherokees, each of whom led a personal war for what he believed in. I have tried to separate the many legends from the facts about these men in an effort to record as true an account of Proctor and Christie as possible.

I am greatly indebted to many persons who have helped make this work possible; in particular to A. D. Lester of Westville, Oklahoma, and Cecil Atchison of Fort Smith, Arkansas. Both men have been avid collectors of data on frontier, Indian nation, and Arkansas border history for many years. Both are considered as perhaps the best authorities on such history, and their research, guidance, opinions, and encouragement have been indispensable to me. Their rapport with the Cherokees and knowledge of eastern Oklahoma also opened the doors for the many personal interviews necessary in establishing a factual account of these last two Cherokee warriors.

# Part One

# EZEKIEL PROCTOR

Zeke Proctor holding his rifle. An original of this photograph is owned by Mrs. Elizabeth Walden. This is the most well-known picture of Zeke since several original prints were distributed among various members of his family and friends.

# I

# The Proctor Family

Ezekiel Proctor was born July 4, 1831, in the Cherokee nation of the state of Georgia, seven years before his family was forced to leave their homeland. He was one-half Cherokee, the son of a white man, William Proctor, and a Cherokee girl named Dicey Downing. Zeke was one of eight known children—Sarah, Elizabeth, Adam, Archibald, Johnson, Rachael, and Nannie. The Proctors, like most Cherokees, were successful farmers.* The Georgia Cherokee nation encompassed good farmland, and many whites of Georgia resented the Indians' control of this land, their nice homes, and their farms. With the discovery of gold on Cherokee lands, the resentment among the whites grew rapidly, and Georgia white citizens put strong pressure on state and federal authorities to move the Indians from their state.

The growing controversy over the removal of all Indians from Georgia, as well as from other states, was a strong political issue in Andrew Jackson's campaign for the presidency. Upon his election in November of 1828, advocates of Indian removal pushed for legislation. After one of the bitterest debates in the history of Congress, the Indian Removal Bill was passed in May of 1830. This bill gave the president power to exchange lands in the West with Indian tribes residing within the boundaries of a state.

* The 1835 Census of the Cherokee Nation East listed the William Proctor family as owning two farms on the Etower River in Georgia.

The Georgia state legislature passed an act declaring Indian Territory within their state to be subject to Georgia state law. This created an opportunity for oppressing the Cherokees, for the Indians had their own laws and constitutional form of government that were in many instances in direct conflict with Georgia state law. Under this act inexhaustible excuses were found to deprive the Indians of their rights and property, and it was hoped by most Georgia whites that this act would encourage the Cherokees to voluntarily leave the state and settle lands to the west. The Cherokee nation sent a delegation to Washington to appeal to President Jackson for protection of their homeland from the threatening Georgia whites. Their appeals were in vain, however, and they were told to encourage their nation to voluntarily leave for new lands in the West.

The Georgia act of 1828 did not recognize any Cherokee law or government body and made it illegal for the Cherokees to hold their council meetings within the Georgia state boundaries. The Indians then found it necessary to move their capital from New Echota, Georgia, to a point in Tennessee known as Red Clay. From here they continued their fight against the state of Georgia, and made many appeals to the Supreme Court and President Jackson for protection of their rights. These actions postponed forcible removal until December 29, 1835. On this date, while their chief, John Ross, was in Washington trying to save the Cherokee nation, a handful of tribal subchiefs were bribed and influenced to sign a treaty authorizing removal. Although President Jackson was aware that these tribal officials did not have authority to speak for the Indian nation and that John Ross was strongly opposed to the treaty when he learned of it, Jackson, because of political pressures, had no choice but to accept it as final.

General Winfield Scott was ordered by the president to take command of federal troops already in the Cherokee nation. He was also authorized to recruit as many additional troops from surrounding states as were needed to carry out the removal. Seven thousand troops in all were employed to implement the president's order to remove some twenty thousand remaining Cherokees. The Indians had been totally disarmed earlier by General Wool and had no means of resistance left. Scott set up headquarters at Fort Butler, Tennessee, and issued a proclamation that emigration must begin at once, and before another moon had passed, every Cherokee man, woman, and child must be in motion towards the West as commanded by the president of the United States.

General Scott's troops were dispersed throughout the nation to evict all Cherokees from their homes and drive them to recently erected stockades to be held for removal. The troops were ordered to shoot any who refused to leave, and many chose death over leaving their homelands for the unknown West. Families were frequently interrupted during their meals and forced out of their homes at bayonet point to the stockades. As they were evicted, their homes, cattle, horses, and personal properties were left to be taken into possession by any one who pleased. This left the Indians without the necessities of life—bedding, cooking utensils, clothing, horses, and food.

Nearly seventeen thousand Cherokees were gathered in stockades. In June, the first twenty-eight hundred were rendezvoused, divided into three detachments, and the long march begun. As a result of the high rate of death and disease reported from the first three marches, the remaining Cherokee council requested General Scott to delay additional removals until fall, or until the long drought was over. They told him they would organize and police their own removal if he would grant this request. General Scott agreed and was strongly criticized by his white associates for granting such permission. The prevailing drought conditions delayed the next removal until early October at which time thirteen thousand, including the Indians' Negro slaves, were divided into detachments of one thousand persons. Each party set up its own officers, laws, and police force. All detachments assembled at Rattlesnake Springs near what is now Charleston, Tennessee. At the final council meetings, held at Red Clay, Tennessee, before the first detachment left, it was decided that their old constitution and laws would continue in their new homeland. The first party to begin the journey was under command of the Cherokee-appointed officer John Benge, and it left on October 1, 1838. Zeke Proctor often mentioned that his family was in the fourth detachment to leave Charleston. According to one of the best works on the Trail of Tears, *Indian Removal* by Grant Foreman (University of Oklahoma Press, Norman, 1966), the John Benge detachment was the fourth party to leave the Georgia Cherokee nation. Therefore it seems reasonable to assume that the Proctor family left their Georgia home with the Benge party.

Mrs. Elizabeth Walden, Zeke Proctor's granddaughter, recalls that he often mentioned the suffering and hardships of this journey. The particular group with whom Zeke and his family left were crowded onto flatboats and made the journey by water while others found it necessary to walk. Zeke frequently told of the many travelers who died and were buried along the riverbanks. The flatboats took Zeke's family to a point near the present Webber's Falls, Oklahoma, where they left the water and journeyed overland to their destination.

The Proctor family settled in the northern portion of the present Adair County, Oklahoma. Their home was where the Johnson cemetery on Oklahoma State Highway 33 is now located. The Johnson cemetery was originally the Proctor family cemetery and is located near their original home. The Cherokees set up districts similar to counties or states within their new nation. The Proctor lands were in the Going Snake District of the Cherokee nation. The district received its name from a full-blooded Cherokee chief who was an eloquent speaker of the old Indian style. His Indian name was Eenah-tah-tah-oo, meaning a snake crawling along, but when translated into English and shortened was called Going Snake. Going Snake and his brother Sleeping Rabbit came up the Trail of Tears in 1837 or 1838, and both died shortly after arriving in Oklahoma. At the age of eighty, Going Snake rode a pony on the trail. He was buried in the Russell community some six miles northeast of the present Westville, Oklahoma.

Zeke Proctor in his Civil War uniform. Note that he is carrying two pistols. His hatband boasts several large rattlers from rattle-snakes he had killed. The original tintype is owned by Mrs. Elizabeth Walden.

This is the only known photograph of Zeke Proctor made without his hat. The original tintype is owned by his granddaughter, Mrs. Elizabeth Walden of Watts, Oklahoma.

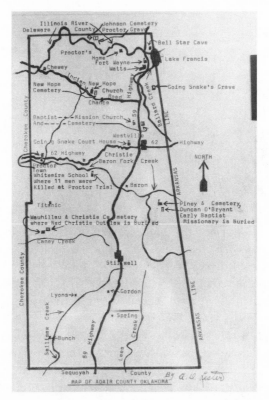

Present Adair County, Oklahoma, is made up of the original Going Snake and Flint districts of the Indian nation. Zeke Proctor's home was in Going Snake District. Points of reference to the Proctor story are indicated.

The handcuffs Zeke Proctor used when he served as sheriff of Going Snake District and as a deputy U.S. marshal. They are owned by Mrs. Elizabeth Walden of Watts, Oklahoma.

# II

## *The Man and His Lawless Environment*

The new lands were strange to the Cherokees, especially to the older members of the tribe who were born in Georgia and had spent their lives there. Many had lost children, mothers, fathers, grandparents, and friends from disease, starvation, or other hardships of their long journey. Families and friends had become separated. The Proctors, like other families, had lost everything and arrived in Oklahoma with scarcely more than the clothes they wore. This was typical of the deprivation that left a great bitterness in the hearts of the Cherokees. It seems unlikely that a boy of only seven could feel the hatred for the white man that Zeke's father and mother must have felt, but no doubt his father often talked of their terrible oppression, and Zeke grew to fear and distrust the white man at an early age.*

Several writers have stated that Zeke committed his first murder by killing a soldier named Wasp with a bow and arrow on the Trail of Tears. There is no factual basis for this story, and is difficult to imagine a seven-year-old boy as a murderer. It has been indicated that Zeke's family left with the fourth group from Georgia, and according to Grant Forman's account in his *Indian Removal* those in charge of this detachment were also Cherokees. It is unreasonable to think

---

* As has been told, William Proctor was white and his wife Indian. Georgia law considered any white man who married an Indian to be Indian, and from that point on he was treated accordingly.

little Zeke would have killed one of his own tribesman. Another writer told a tale of Zeke shooting a playmate out of a tree, and when he was asked why he did it he answered, "To see him fall." A. D. Lester, who has spent many years researching Zeke Proctor's life, shares this writer's opinion that both of these stories of Zeke's boyhood murders are completely untrue.

The Cherokee Council had decided at its last meeting at Red Clay, Tennessee, that its former Georgia constitution and laws would also prevail in the new homeland. The form of the Cherokee government was modeled after that of the United States with legislative, executive, and judicial branches. The Cherokee laws, courts, and tribal procedure were much like those of the white man. They had their own lawyers, judges, court officials, and jury systems. The Cherokee tribe law enforcement agency was known as the Light Horse (Indian police), and their authority extended over the Indian citizens within the tribal territory of the Indian nation. The Light Horse had no authority over the white citizens of the United States.

Arkansas, immediately adjoining the Indian nation to the east and only five miles from the Proctor farm, had gained statehood on June 15, 1836. A federal judicial district was formed and a court established in Little Rock with one judge holding only two sessions annually. In 1830 the Twenty-third Congress had passed the Intercourse Act. This act was to regulate trade and intercourse with Indians and was intended to preserve peace on the frontier. The Little Rock court, being the closest federal court, was given the responsibility of administering the Intercourse Law. The court's limited personnel and funds and the infrequency of its sessions precluded any serious law enforcement along the state's western border or for whites within the Indian nation. Although a military fort had been established at Fort Gibson (Indian nation) in 1824 and at Fort Smith, Arkansas, in 1817, it was not the mission of the military to enforce United

States laws, but rather to protect the United States from Indian uprisings. Lawlessness became so widespread along Arkansas' western boundary and throughout the Indian nation that Congress found it necessary to establish another federal district court for the Western District, March 3, 1851. The court was established at Van Buren, Arkansas, five miles downriver from Fort Smith and given jurisdiction over the Arkansas counties of Benton, Washington, Crawford, Franklin, Johnson, Madison, Carroll, Scott, and Polk. It was also given the former Little Rock court's jurisdiction over all of the Indian nations adjoining the state. Judge Daniel Ringo was given tremendous judicial power by the government, but he made little use of it. The border lawlessness was increasing when the Civil War interrupted court business. Sympathizing with the South, Judge Ringo left his federal bench in 1860. One of the best descriptions of the border situations at the time was pointed out in an editorial by the editor of the Fort Smith *Western Independent:* "It is sickening to the heart to contemplate the increase of crime in the Indian country. It is time Congress took this matter in hand and organized a territory, for if crime continues to increase there so fast, a regiment of the deputy marshals cannot arrest all the murderers."

It was in such an environment that Zeke Proctor grew to manhood. Desperadoes from throughout the United States congregated along the border country of Arkansas and the Indian nation to take advantage of the lawlessness. To survive in such an atmosphere, Zeke found it necessary to learn to handle a weapon at an early age. He became a lightning-quick marksman with both pistol and rifle.

There is only one known record of Zeke Proctor killing anyone—Polly Beck Hilderbrand—an episode described in Chapter IV herein, yet he was accused of many murders in his lifetime. Even his son and granddaughter have told colorful but unsubstantiated stories about his killings. Ezekiel Proctor, Jr., indicated in several interviews that his father had killed twenty-five men in his lifetime and was tried and acquitted sixteen times for crimes. Mrs. Elizabeth Walden related in 1969 that she had always been told that her grandfather found it necessary to remain "on the scout" (in hiding) most of his life after his first killing over an argument his brothers got into. According to Mrs. Walden, when Zeke arrived home one day, his father told him that his brothers Arch and Adam had gone to the Jaybirds' home down the river. He was afraid there would be trouble over an argument they had recently had, and he asked Zeke to go see about them. Arriving at the Jaybirds' home Zeke encountered a heated argument. This trouble soon developed into a gunfight in which Zeke killed two of the Jaybird brothers. It was then that Zeke first found it necessary to go on the scout. Mrs. Walden further stated that he had killed "many" United States marshals when they went after him. It is the opinion of the researcher A. D. Lester that the great number of killings attributed to Proctor is unreasonable and unfounded. Although these statements have come from close relatives of Proctor, it is doubtful that a criminal was brought to trial sixteen times without any remaining record in Fort Smith's federal court or in the Cherokee court records. Probably Zeke did kill several times during his lifetime in protecting his life and property along the lawless Arkansas border, but it is the opinion of this writer and of Mr. Lester that he was not the coldblooded killer these stories would intimate. It is true, however, that if Zeke had been brought to trial for any such crimes in the United States District Court in Van Buren, Arkansas, before the Civil War, these records could have been destroyed, for the courthouse and all of its records burned during the war.

Mrs. Walden is not the only source to describe Zeke's involvement in his brothers' argument and the necessity for him to hide out afterwards. Practically all sources of information declare that Zeke Proctor was constantly alert to arrest and was always heavily armed. Many persons interviewed, who remembered Zeke Proctor in their childhood around the Arkansas border towns of Siloam Springs and Cincinnati, provide generally the same basic description of his personality, appearance, and character. Zeke was a friendly, pleasant, half-breed Indian who wore his hair to his shoulders and stood straight as an arrow. He was very proud and inquisitive; he would sometimes stare and contemplate a new piece of machinery or invention in one of the border-city shops. He was never known to put his back to a door when he was inside a building, and when walking down the street he kept his back to the building, walking sideways so he could have a full view of the street at all times. He was said to have always left town by a different route from the one on which he entered. Obviously he had a strong fear of being ambushed or shot in the back and was extremely alert to danger in all situations.

The best source for Zeke's physical appearance is found in his application for a Civil War pension on which he described himself as being 5 feet 7 inches tall, weighing 186 pounds, having dark complexion, and dark eyes and hair. He also stated on such documents that he was one-half Indian. Although all documents that required Zeke's signature were signed with an X, he did sign his name on his pension application. The signature is almost unreadable, however, and it is therefore assumed that late in life he learned to write in English.

It is hard to imagine how Zeke Proctor could have spent so much time in hiding and at the same time developed his prosperous farm and accumulated his many assets. All those interviewed stated he was a most prosperous farmer, and the census of 1890 indicates he had accumulated large holdings. The 1890 census reveals that he had three dwellings, seven other structures, three farms, one hundred acres enclosed, ninety-four acres in cultivation, one thousand bushels of corn, one hundred bushels of wheat, thirty bushels of apples, twenty-five bushels of peaches, ten bushels of turnips, fifteen bushels of irish potatoes, sixty tons of hay, eighty fruit trees, one hundred hogs, forty cattle, five horses, thirteen sheep, seven goats, eighty-one domestic fowls, seven plows, one machine plow, three farm wagons, two clocks, one sewing machine, one beehive. Such property indicates that he was, in fact, a successful farmer, and it would be impossible to accumulate such property and crop abundance without many years of diligent work.

In later life Zeke went into the sawmill business with John Hargrove, one of the founders and a pioneer merchant of Siloam Springs, Arkansas. Jack Reed, eighty-one years of age, at this writing, of Fayetteville, Arkansas, recalls his father, Jim Reed, often talked of his friendship with Zeke Proctor when Jim Reed was sheriff of Washington County, Arkansas. Mr. Reed's father related that Zeke was always fascinated by a sawmill and would visit the mills around the territory watching them for hours at a time. Later Zeke and Hargrove operated their own sawmill successfully.

When the Civil War broke out, most of the Cherokees were sympathizers with the South since many of them had been slaveowners in their native Georgia. Zeke, however, joined the northern cause. His war record shows he enlisted on July 7, 1862, at a point near the present Baxter Springs, Kansas, and served three years as a private in Company L, Third Regiment of the Indian Home Guard, under the command of Colonel Riley. He was wounded in the shoulder during a battle along the Arkansas border. The reason Zeke chose to serve in the federal army, when most of his friends fought for the Confederacy, is not known. It is conjectural that Zeke didn't believe in slavery because of his lifelong love of freedom.

It seems apparent from the many conflicting accounts of Zeke Proctor's personality obtained from interviews and many other sources of research, that he was a man of complex personality. Although some sources indicated that he was one of the worst desperadoes of his day and was regarded with fear by all those who knew him, others described him as a friendly, peaceable, jovial Indian who was intelligent, spoke both English and Cherokee fluently, and loved children. The latter description usually came from persons who had known Proctor best. Therefore it is the writer's opinion, and that of A. D. Lester, that this view best describes the real Zeke Proctor.

It stands to reason that perhaps those who described him as belligerent and fearsome had seen him when he was on a drinking spree. Indians' bouts with "firewater" are legendary, and Zeke was known to sometimes overindulge in liquor. Many white settlers in the border communities such as Cincinnati and Siloam Springs made fortunes selling whiskey to the Indians for years, and unquestionably, many crimes resulted from wild drunken Indian sprees. Zeke and his family did most of their trading in the community of Cincinnati, Arkansas, and several sources mention that when he drank heavily in a local saloon, he would become loud and boisterous and on several occasions shot up the town with the pair of pearl-handled .45s he always carried. Several times after such a spree he is said to have returned to the shops he damaged and offered to pay for the repairs.

The story is told that while riding his pony home, after a day of drinking, he heard a young girl playing the piano in her home at the edge of town. He stopped his horse and listened for quite some time. When the girl stopped playing, Zeke stormed into the parlor, laid his .45s on the piano, and said, "Play." The frightened girl then continued to play until Zeke left.

Indian prisoners on the steps of Judge Parker's court. Note that some prisoners are in leg irons. Zeke Proctor abhorred the trials of Cherokee in federal courts. He and his followers felt that Cherokee nation citizens should be tried by the Cherokee courts and not by those of the United States. Such objections led to the Cherokee uprising that resulted in a treaty between the United States and Proctor. (Photograph courtesy Cecil Atchison Collection)

Garrison Avenue, Fort Smith, Arkansas, in the early 1890's. (Photograph courtesy Cecil Atchison Collection)

# III

## *Zeke and His Family*

Zeke Proctor married Rebecca Mitchell shortly after the Civil War in 1866, and settled along the Illinois River near the present community of Watts, Oklahoma. The following children were born to them: Charlotte in 1866, Francis in 1870, and triplets Linnie, Minnie and William (Willie) in 1872.

In September of 1872, two months after the birth of the triplets, Rebecca took a wagonload of wool to the wool mill at Shilo, Arkansas. The town of Shilo is called Springdale today. Since Zeke feared arrest by United States marshals in Arkansas, he sent a fourteen-year-old Indian boy with Rebecca. Arriving at the mill, they made camp nearby to await the mill opening the next morning. During the night Rebecca was stricken suddenly with what was then called cramp colera and died. Cramp colera is now believed to have been appendicitis. The boy left the body with nearby residents and rushed home to give Zeke the bad news. Rebecca's brothers then went to Shilo for her body and returned it for burial.

In October of 1876 Zeke married Margaret Denton, a widow. Her maiden name had been Margaret Downing. Civil War pension records indicate that they were married by one Hooley Belle, but when Zeke was asked if there was a record of the marriage, he stated he did not know. Zeke and Margaret, Peggy as she was called, raised his children on the Proctor farm on the Illinois River near Watts, Oklahoma. The couple was not known to have had any children.

During his many years of research on Zeke Proctor and his family, A. D. Lester discovered that Proctor had another family, living on a farm some fifteen miles from him and Margaret. Ezekiel Proctor, Jr., after whom the present town of Proctor, Oklahoma, was named, always claimed Zeke Proctor as his father, yet census records do not show Zeke, Sr., to have lived with Ezekiel, Jr. Ezekiel, Jr.'s mother was Jane Harlan, the daughter of Duncan O'Bryant, the first Baptist missionary teacher to come into the Indian Territory. Census records list the family in 1880 to include Jane Harlan, forty-four, George Harlan, twenty-four, Ellis Harlan, eighteen, and Ezekeil Harlan, twelve. The 1880 census is the only census on which Ezekiel, Jr., is listed as having the last name of Harlan.

During this period it was not uncommon for a Cherokee to have more than one wife at the same time. It also was not considered necessary to perform wedding ceremonies or have legal recordings of marriages. Common-law marriage was a general practice and accepted by Indian law until more rigid marriage laws were adopted by the Cherokee government in later years. Since Ezekiel, Jr., was listed only on one census as a Harlan and on all other censuses as a Proctor, a mistake on the Harlan records seems to have been made. Ezekiel was always told by his mother that Zeke Proctor was his father, and in an interview with A. D. Lester, Zeke, Jr., stated he remembered that his father visited with them often but did not live with them all of the time. On the May 19, 1883, Cherokee headright pay records (to compensate the Cherokees for their Georgia lands, the government made periodic payments) show that Jane Harlan signed for Ezekiel Proctor, Jr.'s allowance of $15.50. On all census records Jane Harlan is listed as white, and all her children are listed as Cherokee. Since Zeke, Sr., listed on his census records that he maintained three dwellings, it is apparent that he had two wives and two families on two separate farms. Jane Harlan's first husband was killed during the Civil War in the battle at Cain Hill, Arkansas, and presumably she became Zeke Proctor's common-law wife thereafter.

Ezekiel Proctor, Jr., lived in what is now Proctor, Oklahoma, and married Sallie Ann Sanders. They had the following children: Samuel, Eli, Charles J., Walter, and Mary J. Walter Proctor, at the time of this writing, lives in Proctor and has one of his grandfather's famous pearl-handled .45s, his rifle, and saddle. Mrs. Elizabeth Walden remembers attending her grandfather Zeke's funeral when she was eleven, and she recalls that his weapons were buried with him according to Indian custom. But since Zeke always carried two .45s, he could have had one buried with him and the other passed along to his family by Jane Harlan.

To further complicate the marriages and family of Zeke Proctor, the Emmit Starr history of the Cherokee lists still another "marriage" to an Eliza Chaney Welch. Since there is no other known record of this marriage, Eliza was undoubtedly another common-law wife. As late as September 24, 1923, Margaret Denton Proctor made application for Zeke's widow's pension. There is no other record of Jane Harlan or Eliza Chaney Welch making a widow's pension application.

Zeke Proctor's triplets, Linnie, Willie, and Minnie. (Photograph courtesy A. D. Lester)

Kermit Beck in front of the old Beck Mill. The mill stands on his property near Flint, Oklahoma. It was at this site that Zeke Proctor shot and killed Polly Beck Hilderbrand. (Photograph by Phillip Steele)

# IV

## *The Beck Mill Incident*

Thomas Beck and his family, like the Proctors, came up the Trail of Tears from Georgia in the 1830s. Beck settled lands along Flint Creek some ten miles west of the present Siloam Springs, Arkansas. Kermit Beck, age sixty-nine at the time of this writing, is Thomas Beck's great-grandson. Kermit lives today on the original Beck lands his ancestor settled. These lands were turned over to the family as their Cherokee allotment when Oklahoma became a state in 1907. The old Beck mill still stands near Kermit Beck's home, and he enjoys relating the interesting history of this mill and the important role it played in the early history of the Cherokee nation and early Oklahoma statehood.

A Frenchman named Towers brought a large buhrstone for grinding wheat and another stone for grinding corn from France to New Orleans in 1845. The buhrstones were shipped by boat up the Mississippi and then up the Arkansas to Fort Gibson, Indian Territory. From Fort Gibson the buhrs were transported by ox team to the mill site on Flint Creek. Towers found the mill construction cost to be more than he could finance alone, and he sold an interest to Thomas Beck. The mill was completed in 1845, and soon it became an important trade center for the Cherokee nation, serving a wide area of the greater Indian nation. The small community that grew up around the mill became known as Beckwith. Today it is known as Flint, Oklahoma.

Before the Civil War, Steve Hilderbrand purchased Tower's share of the mill, and it became known as the Hilderbrand Mill. It is still sometimes referred to by this name. Also before the Civil War, Thomas Beck's son, Aaron Heading Beck, became active in the mill's operation. Aaron Beck, or "Head" Beck, as he was called, was Kermit Beck's grandfather. Hilderbrand soon married "Head" Beck's daughter, Polly.

During the Civil War the mill was captured by Federal forces. Aaron Beck was forced to run the mill for the Union Army and was closely guarded to make sure he didn't escape. Aaron Beck gave his word of honor to the Union Army that he would not escape and would run the mill for them until spring. When spring came he slipped away during the night and joined General Stand Watie's* Confederate forces who were encamped several miles to the south. After the war Aaron Beck returned and resumed operation of his mill. It is not known exactly when Steve Hilderbrand died, but it is generally assumed by his relatives of today that he was killed during the Civil War, leaving Polly Beck Hilderbrand a widow.

Several writers have indicated that Zeke Proctor was related by marriage to Polly and the Beck family. The exact relationship, if any, is not known but is said to have been through the Hilderbrand family. Kermit Beck recalls his father, Tony Beck, and his grandfather, Aaron Beck, mentioning that Aaron and Zeke Proctor were at one time very close friends. They no doubt saw each other frequently since both the Proctors and the Becks were quite influential in early Cherokee government. During the Civil War the Becks were sympathizers with the South, while Zeke Proctor fought with Union forces. No doubt this opposition brought an end to the friendship Beck and Proctor once had.

---

* Stand Watie was the only full-blooded Indian Brigadier General in the Confederate Army. Watie's heroic regiment rendered inestimable service to the Confederate cause. Watie was born December 12, 1806, and died September 9, 1871.

It was during the first few years following the war that Zeke had gained a reputation around the territory as a "bad Indian." He was known to have taken as boarders the Wickliffe brothers, a dangerous outlaw gang, and other known criminals at his farm home near the Arkansas border. His border saloon drinkfests and town shootings had also contributed to his reputation.

Zeke's sister, Susan, was married to Jim Kesterson, a white man. They lived on a farm near what is now Sallisaw, Oklahoma. Upon visiting his sister, Zeke found that Kesterson had left his wife and two children and that they had been without food for several days. Zeke took Susan and her children to another sister's home and vowed he would kill Kesterson on sight if he ever found him. There are several conflicting accounts of the actions Zeke took when he learned that Kesterson was courting the widow Polly Beck Hilderbrand and working at the Beck mill. Three such accounts come from extremely reliable sources, but since all three accounts conflict slightly, the reader must decide which story seems most reasonable.

The first account comes from the Beck family and was passed along to Kermit Beck by the past Beck generations. On his way to the mill to settle his problem with Kesterson, Zeke stopped by one of the border saloons. He got drunk and became enraged at the kidding he received from friends in the saloon. Riding hard to the Beck mill, he found Kesterson and Polly outside the mill. He stopped his horse some distance away before he was seen and yelled out to Kesterson, as he drew his .45s, "I'm going to kill me a white man." Before Kesterson could take cover, Zeke's gun roared. Just as the shot was fired, Polly jumped in front of her lover and caught the deadly bullet in her chest. Zeke fired two more shots at Kesterson as he ran into the mill, and one bullet slightly wounded him. Realizing he had accidentally killed the daughter of his relative and good friend Aaron Beck, Zeke fled in confusion. According to the Beck account, Zeke

stayed in hiding for several months before he was convinced
by friends to turn himself in to the Indian Light Horse
authorities.

In 1930 Elizabeth Walden wrote a slightly different account of the Beck mill shooting in a paper she wrote about
her grandfather and entered in an Oklahoma history contest
sponsored by the Works Project Administration. She described the shooting as follows: On a morning in February,
1872, Zeke, his wife Rebecca and children Charlotte and
Francis drove an ox team to the home of his brother-in-law,
Charley Allen on Mose Prairie near the Beck mill. Leaving
his family at Mose Prairie, he went alone to the mill where,
she said, the shooting occurred much as the Becks described
it. After the shooting Zeke told his family what he had done
and then rode directly to the home of Jack Wright, sheriff
of Going Snake District, and turned himself in. Wright then
placed him under guard to be held for trial.

The third account was related by Eli Whitmire to a
reporter for the Adair County *Oklahoma Democrat-Gleaner* in
1939. Whitmire was thirteen at the time of the Proctor shooting and later became a brother-in-law to Jack Wright, the
sheriff of Going Snake District, who had arrested Proctor.
This account states that Zeke saddled his pony one morning
in February, 1872, and left alone for the Beck mill some ten
miles away. Arriving at the mill he bade Kesterson and Polly
good morning. Soon their conversation drifted into a heated
argument. Kesterson reached for his gun, but Zeke, being
much quicker, beat him to the draw. Polly, who had been
trying to prevent the argument between them, jumped in
front of Kesterson just as Zeke's .45 discharged, and she
caught the bullet in her chest. Zeke then fired two more shots
at Kesterson, putting two holes in his coat as he fled to the
second floor of the mill. Zeke returned home and immediately sent a message to Sheriff Wright. Wright then sent guards
to Zeke's home to guard him until his trial could be set.

The above accounts do not mention the exact date on

which Zeke shot at Kesterson at the Beck mill. However, this date is shown clearly on the United States commissioner's documents of the Western District of Arkansas. The document requesting the U.S. marshal to arrest Proctor states as follows:

UNITED STATES OF AMERICA
  Western District of Arkansas
TO THE MARSHAL OF THE WESTERN
DISTRICT OF ARKANSAS
GREETINGS:

Whereas, complaint on oath hath been made before me, charging that Ezekiel Proctor did on the 13th day of February A.D. 1872 in the Western District of Arkansas, and in the Indian Country commit an assault with intent to kill, with a deadly weapon J. J. Kesterson a white man contrary to the form of the Statute in such cases made and provided, and against the peace and dignity of the United States. Now, therefore, you are hereby commanded, in the name of the President of the United States of America, to apprehend the said Ezekiel Proctor and bring his body forthwith before me J. W. O. Churchill a commissioner appointed by the United States District Court for said District, whenever he may be found, that he may then and there be dealt with according to law for said offence.

Given under my hand this 11th day of April A.D. 1872 in the 96th year of our independence.

J. W. O. Churchill
U.S. COMMISSIONER—
WESTERN DISTRICT ARKANSAS

The above document was presented to the United States marshal, Logan Roots, and the difficulties Deputy Marshal Owens and Peevy experienced in trying to apprehend Proctor are outlined in Chapter V.

A number of writers have indicated that Zeke was held in the Saline District Cherokee jail until trial, but there is no substantial evidence of this. It was a custom of Cherokee law not to imprison offenders. The Light Horse police were assigned to guard the accused until the trial date and were paid fifty cents per day for doing so. The prisoner was generally free to remain at his home or go about his daily affairs but was continuously under guard. When trial dates were set, the guards were responsible for getting the prisoner safely to the courtroom at the assigned time. The Cherokee lawbreaker was also on a sort of honor system. Once arrested it was considered most dishonorable to attempt escape, for then the system would have failed. As a result few prisoners were ever imprisoned under Cherokee law, and few tried to escape while awaiting trial under a home guard.

The above accounts of the shooting are similar, with the exception of the Becks' which claimed that Proctor was in hiding for several months after the shooting. Zeke's granddaughter, Elizabeth Walden, and Eli Whitmire stated that the shooting occurred in February of 1872. The commissioner's document states the assault occurred February 13. If these dates were correct, Proctor could not have spent any length of time in hiding since the first trial date was originally set in March of 1872. Therefore, it is the opinion of this writer and of A. D. Lester that Zeke immediately reported his crime to the sheriff, Jack Wright.

# V

## The Trial

The Treaty of 1866 gave the Indian nations the right of authority over all crimes between Indians, and between Indians and "adopted" white citizens living within their jurisdiction. Polly Beck Hilderbrand was half Cherokee. The Cherokee authorities considered Kesterson, who was white, an adopted citizen of the Cherokee nation. The United States District Court for the Western District of Arkansas had jurisdiction over crimes between Indians and white citizens of the United States as well as between white citizens who might be in Indian territory but not considered adopted citizens of the Indian nation.

On March 3, 1871, Congress approved an act authorizing the Western District to be moved from Van Buren, Arkansas, to Fort Smith, Arkansas. This act also authorized the movement of the marshal, district attorney, judge, and court clerk offices to Fort Smith. Henry J. Caldwell, then judge of Arkansas' Eastern District federal court located at Little Rock, was appointed by President Grant to preside over the Fort Smith court and to assume the court's responsibilities of the vast Indian Territory to the west. Logan H. Roots was appointed United States marshal. Judge Caldwell, like his predecessor Judge Ringo, was relatively ineffective in controlling the tremendous increase in crime throughout the Indian nation.

More and more white settlers were moving into the Indian nations to find jobs in railroad construction or to trade with the Indians. Outlaw gangs and the worst of men from all parts of the nation were using to their advantage the lawlessness of the Indian Territory. Many crimes involving white men not considered adopted citizens went unpunished as a result of the lack of proper law enforcement by the Fort Smith court and the lack of authority the Indian police had over the white men in their territory. On the other hand, when an Indian was accused in federal court of a crime against a white man, marshals were sent out immediately to capture the Indian and drag him to the Fort Smith court. The white man's language and his court were strange to the red man, and the Indians felt that the court would always find him guilty simply because he was an Indian and therefore a "bad Indian." The Cherokees saw many of their friends and loved ones dragged to Fort Smith never to return. Some were guilty; some were not. The Cherokee government felt their citizens would receive a fairer trial under their jurisdiction. As a result of this interference by the federal court in their nation, a great fear and strong resentment against the United States grew among the Indians. The Indians felt that their government should have absolute and total authority in their nation whether the parties were white or Indian, citizens or adopted citizens of the Indian nation. The resentment continued to grow under Judge William Story who succeeded Caldwell in 1872.

The Beck family was very large and influential in the Indian nation. Outraged over the shooting of their "Aunt Polly," the Becks were determined to see Zeke Proctor hang. The Proctor family was also quite influential among the Cherokees, and both families had many friends and relatives in Cherokee government positions.

Zeke was one of the leaders in the Keetoowa Society, which was started during this era by conservative Cherokees. The society, which exists today, originally began as a religious resistance movement. As American citizens began crowding into the Cherokee nation, the Keetoowa Society was formed with the purpose of preserving the nation's right of independence, tribal customs, and traditions.

Followers of the Keetoowa Society, like many Indian religions, believed in little people, or fairies—both good and evil. The good fairies protected and helped those who were in favor with them; the bad or evil fairies were mischievous and harmful to humans. In times of trouble a Cherokee would go to the top of the highest mountain he could find and pray for the assistance and guidance of the good fairies. The order also believed that some men had power over these little people, were in constant favor of the good fairies, and could keep them nearby at all times. The belief that Zeke Proctor was one of these men greatly contributed to his recognition as a leader among his people.

The Keetoowa Society was often referred to as the Pin Indian Organization. This name derived from the pin made from two crossed feathers that the members wore on their clothing or saddle blankets. The pin signified that through their Keetoowa Society membership they were strong supporters of the Cherokee national government, principles, and treaty rights of independence from America. Also, the pin warned that strong reprisals would be taken against anyone who harmed a member of the religious order.

The Keetoowa organization was one of the main groups denouncing federal authority of any kind within their nation, firmly opposing the federal court, and strongly favoring their own law enforcement and judicial system. The Pin member took a pledge that he would not testify against any party in U.S. federal court for a crime he had witnessed. Proctor therefore had many supporters and friends throughout the Indian nation and in the courts. This caused the Beck family to fear the Cherokee court's ability to assemble a jury that would find anything but acquittal for Zeke. The Becks then strove to delay his trial in any way possible, hoping to get the federal court in Fort Smith to intervene in the case before the Cherokees brought Zeke to trial. The Becks were sure that if Zeke could be tried in federal court he would be sentenced to death, for few Indians accused of murder had ever been acquitted by the Fort Smith court.

The Cherokee authorities, realizing that the Becks might be successful in getting federal intervention, immediately set an early trial date. The Beck's prosecuting attorney was successful in having Jim Walker ruled ineligible to try the case because he was related to Proctor. This made it necessary for Cherokee Chief Louis Downing to call a council meeting to discuss the case and to appoint another judge. The council met as quickly as possible and appointed Thomas Wolf as judge, but Wolf received so much pressure from both the Beck and Proctor factions that he resigned and refused to try the case. This gave the Becks still more time before the council could meet again. Chief Downing then appointed Blackhaw Sixkiller judge for the case. Again, the Becks, through the prosecuting attorney, attempted to further delay the trial by pointing out that Sixkiller was a friend of Proctors and could not give Proctor an objective judgment. The council again met to consider the Beck complaint but ruled that Sixkiller would be the judge.

The trial had originally been set to be held in the Going Snake District courthouse, which was located on Peacheater Creek or Barron Fork Creek west of the present Westville, Oklahoma. Realizing the strong tension that existed between both the Beck family supporters and Proctor supporters throughout the nation and the possibility of one or both factions trying to disrupt the court's proceedings, Chief Downing moved the place of trial from the Going Snake District courthouse to the Whitmire schoolhouse near the present community of Christie, Oklahoma. There were most likely two reasons for this move. First, the Whitmire school was farther from the region in which most of the Beck family and its supporters lived. Second, and probably the best reason, was the fact that the Whitmire school could be more closely guarded since it had only one window and one door and was built of sturdy logs. Both exits could easily be secured in the event there was an attempt to disrupt the court's proceedings while in session. The Going Snake District courthouse had many doors and windows, and it would have been difficult to secure all accesses to the building. The trial was set for April 15, 1872.

On April 11 Kesterson and several of the Becks went to Fort Smith and filed charges against Proctor before U.S. Commissioner James O. Churchill. Churchill issued warrants for the arrest of Proctor, Soldier Sixkiller, Red Bird Sixkiller, Thomas Walkingstick, John Creek, Isaac Vann, Ellis Foreman, Joe Chaney, and the entire jury. Deputy Marshals Joe G. Peavy and Jacob G. Owens were assigned to issue the warrants and were instructed not to serve the warrants if Proctor was found guilty. If acquitted, they were to serve the warrants and bring in all parties for questioning in the Fort Smith court.

As with other segments of Proctor's life, there are many conflicting accounts of the trial's proceedings. Since Eli Whitmire was present at the trial when he was thirteen, and observed firsthand the events of April 15, 1872, his account as related to the Adair County *Democrat-Gleaner* in 1939 is considered to be the most reliable. When the court convened Judge B H. (Cornick) Sixkiller sat at a small wooden table at the rear of the schoolhouse facing the door to the west. Joe Starr, the court clerk, sat immediately to the judge's left and Mose Alberty, Proctor's attorney, sat to the judge's right. Proctor was sitting next to his attorney and one of his guards, Tom Walkingstick, stood near him.

The small schoolhouse was jammed full of spectators, and hundreds of others who could not get in the courtroom surrounded the building outside. Four guards were posted outside the door to prevent anyone from forcibly interrupting the trial. These guards were Lincoln England, John Looney,

John Walkingstick, and Jesse Shill. While the prosecuting attorney, Johnson Spake, was arguing a motion before the court, Deputy Marshals Peavy and Owens arrived with a posse that had accompanied them from Fort Smith. Marshal Owens had instructed the posse not to try to enter the courtroom and to remain peaceably outside until the court's decision was made. The posse consisted of Kesterson, White Sut Beck, several others of the Beck family, and their friends. As the posse approached the school White Sut Beck appeared to take over command of the group and was joined by other members of the Beck family and their friends who were all heavily armed and waiting outside the school building. Sut Beck leveled his double-barreled shotgun at the guards by the door and demanded they step aside. The group then burst into the courtroom, guns in hand. Sut Beck immediately aimed his shotgun at Zeke. Johnson Proctor, Zeke's brother, grabbed the gun's barrel just as it fired and received the full charge in the breast. The second shot struck Zeke in the knee. Pandemonium then broke out as the Beck and Proctor factions fired wildly. For a while it seemed a duel to the death. What was left of the posse was forced to run as they were overpowered by the guns on the Proctor side, the Indian police, and spectators around the building. When the smoke cleared the dead and wounded covered the ground in front of the little log schoolhouse. Nine men had been killed in the battle and two were mortally wounded. An undetermined number of others received minor wounds. Those killed on the Proctor side were Johnson Proctor and Mose Alberty, Zeke's attorney.

Alberty had been sitting on the judge's desk when he was struck by a bullet. On the Beck side those killed were Sam Beck, Black Sut Beck, William Hicks, Riley Woods, George Selvage and James Ward. Deputy U.S. Marshal Owens and Bill Beck were mortally wounded in the battle and died a short time afterwards. Marshal Owens stated, as he lay dying, that he tried to stop the battle but could not. Those wounded on the Proctor side were the presiding judge, B. H. (Cornick) Sixkiller, Zeke Proctor, Ellis Foreman (a juror), Joseph Churver (a juror), Deputy Sheriffs John Proctor,* Isaac Vann, and Palone.

Eli Whitmire related that he and his brother Steve Whitmire were instructed by their mother, who was a widow, to hitch up the mules to their wagon. The boys then drove to the school where Zeke and his followers helped load the dead and wounded into the wagon. Driving to the Whitmire home a short distance away, the dead were laid out on a large front porch until their relatives came to get the bodies. The wounded were taken inside where they were treated by Mrs. Whitmire and relatives.

Kermit Beck described the events as follows: His grandfather, Aaron Beck, was at the time the head of the Beck family. He had tried to discourage the Becks from going to the courthouse, armed or otherwise, and suggested they leave the situation in the hands of the authorities. Aaron Beck, who, as pointed out earlier, had at one time been a close friend of Zeke Proctor, did not go himself, and he feared that if his family showed up at the school, lives would be lost.

Fearing that a large posse would return from Fort Smith before Zeke's trial could be finished, the judge rushed up proceedings. The next day Zeke was taken to Captain Arch Scraper's home nearby, and court convened early. They did not go back to the school, for they knew that if a posse from Fort Smith did return, they would go to the school first. The court's jury of twelve men quickly found Zeke Proctor "not guilty" and adjourned.

* John Proctor was from another Proctor family not related to Zeke.

The Federal court building at Fort Smith as it appeared during Parker's service as judge. Note the prison wagon near the steps. These wagons were used by marshals to bring prisoners from the Indian Territory. This is one of the earliest known photographs of the building. (Photograph courtesy Cecil Atchison Collection)

The early town of Fort Smith, Arkansas, as it looked from the fort. The town began to grow up soon after the fort completion in 1842. This is one of the earliest known photographs of early Fort Smith. (Photograph courtesy Cecil Atchison Collection)

# VI

## Amnesty and Zeke's Treaty with the United States

News of the tragedy at Whitmire school spread rapidly throughout the Indian nation and was looked upon by the Indians as an attack by the United States government authorities. The bitterness of the Indians grew even more rapidly as a result of the intervention in their judicial system by the federal court in Fort Smith. The jurors in Proctor's case no doubt were strongly swayed by the attempt to disrupt their nation's judicial procedures, and Zeke Proctor, already a leader within the Pin Indian organization, now became greatly admired throughout the territory for the defeat of the marshal-led posse attacking an Indian court. Zeke, as a fugitive, became a martyr in the Cherokee cause for total independence in government and law enforcement within their nation.

After the trial Zeke feared he would be blamed for the death of Deputy Marshal Owens and the others who died during the courtroom battle. He felt the Fort Smith court would be sending out more marshals and a larger posse to bring him in for trial in federal court. He also knew that in the event he was captured and tried in Fort Smith, he would surely hang, for the federal court would use him to prove a point of authority over the Indian nation. Zeke, therefore, went into hiding. Research also indicates that as many as fifty or more men accompanied him, and no doubt all were members of the Pin. Although this band of men was heavily armed, it was not an outlaw gang and had the full support of the Cherokee government and lawmen. The mission of the group was not only to protect Zeke Proctor from possible capture by United States marshals but also to discourage the U.S. federal court from exercising any authority within the Indian nation. The Cherokee nation felt that the treaty of 1866 giving them the right of self-government had been violated by the interference of the United States Marshals Owens and Peavy. Zeke and his followers, therefore, had the support of the entire Cherokee nation, with the possible exception of the Beck family.

On Wednesday, April 17, shortly after Proctor's trial had adjourned, a posse of some twenty to twenty-five men under the command of Deputy United States Marshal C. F. Robinson arrived at the Whitmire home. Dr. Julian C. Fields and Dr. C. F. Pierce accompanied the party from Fort Smith and treated the wounded from the previous day's battle. Marshal Robinson had been instructed by the Fort Smith court to bring in Proctor and all of the parties involved in the shooting of Deputies Owens and Peavy. Learning that Proctor and some fifty armed men had retreated to the mountains, he felt it would not be wise to encounter the band with his small posse. He then proceeded to Tahlequah, capital of the Indian nation, and on Thursday, April 18, made the following written request of Chief Louis Downing:

> Dear Sir: I have the honor to demand the surrender of the following named citizens of the Cherokee nation. Said parties were concerned in the attack made on Deputy United States Marshals J. G. Owens and Peavy, and their posse comitatus, at Going Snake district courthouse: Jesse Shill, Ezekiel Proctor, Soldier Sixkiller, One Sixkiller, Thomas Walkingstick, John Creek, John Proctor, Isaac Vann, Ellis Foreman, Joe Chaney, and the jury that was impaneled to try Ezekiel Proctor.

> Yours very respectfully,
> CHARLES F. ROBINSON
> Deputy U.S. Marshal

Chief Downing considered the Proctor case closed since the accused had been duly tried in his court of law and found not guilty. He felt the request Robinson made was a further infraction on the Indians' treaty and rights to govern their own nation. Letters of appeal immediately went out to the Cherokee nation delegation in Washington, D.C. (Will P. Ross, William Penn Adair, and C. N. Vann), requesting their help in restoring the Cherokee's treaty rights of self-government, judicial powers, and law enforcement within their own nation.

At the same time, United States Marshal Logan H. Roots of the Fort Smith federal court and the United States district attorney, James H. Huckleberry, were appealing to the attorney general in Washington, George H. Williams, for support and help in administering the Fort Smith court's jurisdiction in regard to the Proctor case in the Cherokee nation. It was even suggested in one letter that federal troops from Fort Sill be deployed to encounter Proctor and his followers.

Both factions soon were successful in bringing their appeals to the attention of Congress. President U. S. Grant also took personal interest in the Proctor case, and during the lengthy debates in Congress concerning the matter, Grant sent the following letter of recommendation to Congress.

HOUSE OF REPRESENTATIVES      Ex Dec.
42nd Congress—Second Session      No. 287

SUBJECT: THE PROCTOR TRIAL—DIFFICULTIES
    IN CHEROKEE COUNTRY

MESSAGE: FROM THE PRESIDENT OF THE
    UNITED STATES

IN ANSWER TO A RESOLUTION OF THE HOUSE
    OF REPRESENTATIVES OF APRIL 29,

RELATIVE TO THE RECENT DIFFICULTIES IN
    THE CHEROKEE COUNTRY.

May 2, 1872—Referred to the Committee on the Judiciary
and ordered to be printed.

To the Speaker of the House of Representatives:

I herewith communicate to the House of Representatives
a report of this date, from the Acting Secretary of the Interi-
or, in answer to the resolution of that body adopted on the
29th ultimo, calling for information relative to the recent
affray at the courthouse in Going Snake District, Indian
Territory.

In view of the feeling of hostility which exists between the
Cherokees and the United States authorities of the Western
District of Arkansas, it seems to be necessary that Congress
should adopt such measures as will tend to allay that feeling
and at the same time secure the enforcement of the laws in
that territory.

I therefore concur with the Acting Secretary of the Interi-
or in suggesting the adoption of a pending bill for the erection
of a United States judicial district within the Indian Territory as a measure which will afford the most immediate remedy
for the existing troubles.

Executive Mansion, May 10, 1872        U. S. GRANT

The Cherokees were, of course, strongly opposed to the
president's suggestion. They did not want any federal court
within their nation. They wanted only protection of their
rights of self-government as outlined in their treaty with the
United States. Over the next several months extreme tension
existed between the Cherokees and the United States. Many
white citizens of the United States traveling through the
Indian nation were mistaken for U.S. marshals and killed.
During this period several marshals working out of Fort
Smith in the performance of their regular duties were sent
into the Indian nation and never heard from again. Zeke
Proctor was usually accused of killing them. There are no
records regarding these killings, but Elizabeth Walden mentioned, in her account of her grandfather's life, that many of

his twenty-five alleged killings occurred during this period. They could very well have been committed by some of the hundreds of Proctor sympathizers or members of the Pin. The number of men killed or the number Zeke Proctor killed, if any, during this period of extreme tension is not known.

The Cherokee delegation in Washington lobbied strongly for the Proctor and the Cherokee cause throughout the next year and were finally successful in obtaining from President Grant total amnesty for Proctor and his followers. Zeke's grandchildren recall that Zeke displayed his amnesty or treaty prominently on a wall of his home for many years. His grandchildren also recall he often talked about his treaty with America.

Inquiry has been made to all known Proctor relatives as to the whereabouts of this original document with no success. Congressional records during this time, President Grant's letters, and Justice Department records do not refer to the amnesty. Many of the Fort Smith federal court records for the period are filed at the Federal Records Center in Fort Worth, Texas. Although there was no treaty document found in these files, the date of the amnesty was indicated by an entry in the court's record book on August 13, 1873.

On June 10, 1873, the federal court grand jury was empaneled, and copies of the original charges made against Proctor and his followers were ordered for presentation to the grand jury. These charges read as follows:

United States of America
Western District of Arkansas.

In the District Court of the United States of America for the Western District of Arkansas. May Term A.D. 1873.

The Grand Jurors of the United States of America duly selected empaneled sworn and charged to inquire in and for the body of the Western District of Arkansas upon their oath do present that Ezekiel Proctor, Arch Scraper, Tail Sixkiller,

Blackhaw Sixkiller, John Walker, Joseph Chaney, George Shill, Jesse Shill, Edwin Downing, Jim Beemer, John Walkingstick, John Creek, John Proctor, Mike Mitchell, Thomas Walkingstick, Ellis Foreman, Nelse Foreman, John Shill, Isaac Vann, Ned Still, and John Looney with force and arms on the 1st day of March A.D. 1872 at the Indian Country in the Western District of Arkansas aforesaid in and upon Jacob Owens a white man and not an Indian then and there being feloniously willfully and of their malice aforethought did make an assault, and that the said Ezekiel Proctor a certain pistol then and there loaded and charged with gunpowder and twenty leaden bullets which pistol he the said Ezekiel Proctor in his right hand then and there had and held to against and upon the said Jacob Owens then and there feloniously willfully and of his malice aforethought did shoot and discharge; and that the said Ezekiel Proctor with the leaden bullets aforesaid out of the pistol aforesaid then and there by force of the gunpowder shot and sent forth as aforesaid Jacob Owens in and upon the left side of him and the said Jacob Owens then and there feloniously willfully and of his malice aforethought did strike penetrate and wound giving to the said Jacob Owens then and there with the leaden bullets aforesaid so as aforesaid shot discharged and sent forth out of the pistol aforesaid by the said Ezekiel Proctor in and upon the left side of him the said Jacob Owens one mortal wound of the depth of six inches and of the breadth of half an inch of which said mortal wound he the said Jacob Owens then and there instantly died. And that the aforesaid Arch Scraper, Tail Sixkiller, Blackhaw Sixkiller, John Walker, Joseph Chaney, George Shill, Jesse Shill, Edwin Downing, Jim Beemer, John Walkingstick, John Creek, John Proctor, Mike Mitchell, Thomas Walkingstick, Ellis Foreman, Nelse Foreman, John Shill, Isaac Vann, Ned Still, and John Looney then and there feloniously willfully and of their malice aforethought were present aiding helping abetting and comforting assisting and maintaining the said Ezekiel Proctor the felony and murder aforesaid in manner and form aforesaid to do and commit. And so the Jurors aforesaid upon their oath aforesaid do say that the said Ezekiel Proctor, Arch Scraper,

Tail Sixkiller, Blackhaw Sixkiller, John Walker, Joseph Chaney, George Shill, Jesse Shill, Edwin Downing, Jim Beemer, John Walkingstick, John Creek, John Proctor, Mike Mitchell, Thomas Walkingstick, Ellis Foreman, Nelse Foreman, John Shill, Isaac Vann, Ned Still, and John Looney him the said Jacob Owens in manner and by the means aforesaid feloniously willfully and of their malice aforethought did kill and murder.

Contrary to the form of the Statute in such cases made and provided and against the peace and dignity of the United States of America.

JAMES H. HUCKLEBERRY
U.S. Attorney

Witnessed By:

| | |
|---|---|
| Joseph Vannoy | Joseph Peevy (deputy marshal) |
| Jas. Hawkins | Paul Jones |
| W. F. Morris | George McLaughlin |
| One Mack | Joseph Starr |
| J. A. Scales | James Kesterson |
| Ezekiel Beck | White Sut Beck |
| John Wright | Five Shannon |
| W. S. Mack | Jeff Beck |
| Sut Beck | W. Ballard |
| John Sturdivant | George Runn |
| T. Spade | Capt. J. W. Churchill |

Similar charges to the above were also made against these men for the killing of Riley Woods, James Ward, and George Selvege.

These charges were originally reviewed by the grand jury in May of 1872, and copies were ordered for an additional review of the case in June of 1873. Since many of the court records are missing, it can only be assumed that President Grant found it to be necessary to grant Proctor and his followers a complete pardon in order to restore peace between the United States and the Indian nation. A letter or document granting this pardon was no doubt issued and reviewed by the grand jury on June 10, 1873.

The Fort Smith court record book indicated that on August 14, 1873, Zeke and his followers were present at a hearing granting each of them total amnesty of their crimes against the United States. The court's entry for this day reads as follows:

Indictment for Murder
United States vs.
Ezekiel Proctor, Arch Scraper, Tail Sixkiller, Blackhaw Sixkiller, John Walker, Joseph Chaney, George Shill, Jesse Shill, Edwin Downing, Jim Beemer, John Walkingstick, John Creek, John Proctor, Mike Mitchell, Thomas Walkingstick, Ellis Foreman, Nelse Foreman, John Shill, Isaac Vann, Ned Still, and John Looney.

Now on this day came the United States of America by V. J. Temple Esq. Attorney for the Western District of Arkansas and made known to the court here that they are unwilling further to prosecute said indictment against the said defendants and with the consent of the Court elect to take a Nolle Prosequi herein. Whereupon the premises being seen and by the Court well and sufficiently understood it is ordered that said defendants be discharged of and from said indictments and their recognizance and go hence without delay.

The above court record is the only mention of the amnesty. Many of the court records are missing, however, and it can only be assumed that the document issued by President Grant and presented to the court on this date has been lost with time. Congressman Ed Edmondson inquired of the Proctor amnesty through several government agencies in Washington and reported to A. D. Lester in his letter of November 8, 1967, the following: "Since records of the 19th Century were very incomplete, it is possible that a newspaper clipping will be the most reliable source of news of this type. They cannot find records of this specific grant of amnesty, and said that an inquiry to the National Archives by them turned up no records on it there. The Library of Congress said that a news clipping often was the most reliable record in those days, and they also advised that you should use it as your substantiation for the grant."

Over the years hundreds of newspaper articles stated that Zeke Proctor was granted amnesty by President Grant. A typical newsstory of Proctor's amnesty was published in the Muskogee (Oklahoma) *News* at the time of Zeke's death. The story appeared as follows in the March 10, 1907 issue: "For years the Proctors evaded every attempt U.S. marshals made to capture them. The people who lived in the Cherokee hills were in sympathy with the Proctor faction and the marshals didn't dare bring the matter to an open contest. The Proctors were never taken and they did not lay down their arms until they were each and every member granted amnesty by President Grant."

Records indicate that Zeke lived up to his agreement with the United States throughout the rest of his life. As a result of his popularity for his past courageous stand against U.S. authority, he was elected to several high positions within the Cherokee government in the years to follow. The Emmit Starr history of the Cherokees declares that Zeke was elected senator from the Going Snake District in 1877 and served in this capacity and other government positions for several years. Proctor had been elected sheriff of the district in 1867 for a short period, and in 1894 he was again elected sheriff.

As mentioned in earlier chapters, the relatively ineffective Fort Smith court's law enforcement within the Indian nation had created a lawless region that was being used to advantage by outlaws and desperadoes, and the situation had become worse during the Proctor controversy. On May 2, 1875, President Grant appointed Isaac C. Parker to the bench at Fort Smith's federal court with instructions to restore law and order in this lawless land. Parker was to spend the next twenty-one years there and during his term of office became known as the "hanging judge" because of some seventy-nine men he sent to the gallows. The Fort Smith federal court records state that Zeke Proctor served as a deputy U.S. marshal and took the oath of office on November 20, 1891, and again on February 12, 1895. Zeke's knowledge of the Indian Territory and its many hideouts provided an invaluable service to the Fort Smith court in bringing many criminals to justice during this period.

After a lengthy siege of pneumonia, Zeke Proctor died at his home on the Illinois River at the age of seventy-six on February 28, 1907. He was buried in the Proctor family cemetery, which is now called the Johnson cemetery, five miles west of Siloam Springs, Arkansas, on Oklahoma State Highway 33. His many friends throughout the Indian nation paid final tribute to Zeke by erecting a large monument that remains today the largest in the Johnson cemetery.

The circumstances that surrounded this half-breed Indian, the deaths of eleven men during his trial, and an eventual amnesty or treaty with the United States make Zeke Proctor one of America's most colorful frontier personalities. Debates among frontier historians as to whether Zeke Proctor should be remembered as a notorious outlaw, persecuted Indian, or martyr for the Cherokee cause will no doubt continue. Although he distinguished himself as a leader within the Cherokee nation's government, he will be best remembered by the Cherokees for his courageous stand against United States authority in an effort to secure the right of self-government for a proud people.

Judge Isaac C. Parker became known as the "hanging judge" because of the some seventy-nine men hanged from his gallows. On one occasion five men were hanged at one time. Judge Parker was appointed federal judge for the district and circuit courts for the Western District of Arkansas, which had criminal jurisdiction over the Indian Territory, on August 10, 1875. He was appointed to the position by President U.S. Grant and served for twenty years. Parker died at his home in Fort Smith, Arkansas, on November 17, 1896.

Judge William Henry Harrison Clayton preceded Isaac Parker as judge for the federal court in the Western District of Arkansas. (Photograph courtesy Cecil Atchison Collection)

Zeke Proctor's tombstone is the largest in the Johnson cemetery, located on Oklahoma State Highway 33, five miles west of Siloam Springs, Arkansas.

The gallows at Parker's court from which seventy-nine men were hanged during his twenty years on the bench at Fort Smith's federal court. (Photograph by Phillip Steele)

George Malledon, Judge Isaac Parker's hangman. Malledon hanged the seventy-nine men Parker sentenced to death. Malledon also designed and built the gallows, shown among these illustrations, that would handle six hangings at one time, and on two occasions it functioned to its maximum capacity. Malledon was also considered to be a master at tying the hangman's knot, whereby the criminal would be killed instantly when the gallows trap dropped. Before each hanging, Malledon would await the nod from Judge Parker, who would be watching from a window in the nearby federal court building. (Photograph courtesy Cecil Atchison Collection)

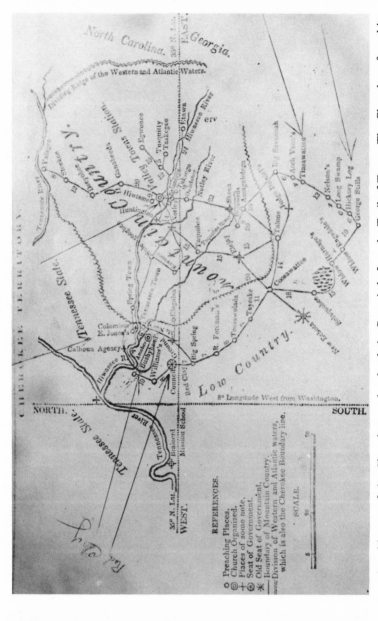

An old map of the Cherokee nation lands in Georgia before the Trail of Tears. The Cherokees found it necessary to move their capital from New Echota, Georgia to Red Clay which was just across the line in Tennessee.

# VII

## *Best-Known Proctor Fables*

There are almost as many legends and stories of Zeke Proctor's deeds as there are families residing in eastern Oklahoma today. Hundreds of stories have been told about him, and over the years these stories have become altered to such an extent that it is almost impossible to separate fact from legend. Although there is little if any basis of fact for these tales, the reader may find them interesting.

### ZEKE THE SUPERHUMAN

Zeke survived the bloody battle that occurred during his trial with only a minor leg wound. He was successful in eluding federal marshals for years and was involved in many shootings. His name was connected with twenty-five or more killings during his lifetime. He participated in many Civil War battles and received only a superficial arm wound. Among the Indians, Zeke gained a reputation of possessing superhuman powers and was believed to carry with him God's protection wherever he went. Zeke's followers liked to stay close to him in hopes this supernatural protection would also protect those near him.

It is doubtful that Zeke had such powers, but from all accounts, it does appear that he did have an uncanny ability to sense danger. He was extra cautious at all times, and this cautiousness, as well as his ability to handle his weapons, no doubt saved him from death on many occasions.

Some accounts indicate that Zeke's secret of survival was the fact that he always wore a metal breastplate beneath his shirt. Other stories claim that Zeke had trained his horse, Faithful, to sense danger and warn him when someone was near. During his many years on the scout it was impossible for anyone to sneak up on his campsite without Zeke knowing it because his horse would awaken him when he detected the slightest sound.

## INDIAN GRAVE HOLLOW

Kermit Beck related a story he recalled that his grandfather Aaron Beck often told. Zeke once told Aaron that he had been accused of many murders in his lifetime but had only killed one time without reason. All his killings had been in self-defense or were accidental, he said, with the exception of the killing of a young Indian. One day while Zeke was riding through a valley near the Illinois River he met the young boy who was carrying a jug of whiskey. Zeke asked the boy for a drink; the boy wouldn't give it to him, so Zeke killed him, took his jug, and buried the Indian where he fell. From that time to this, the valley has been referred to as Indian Grave Hollow.

## THE AUCTION INCIDENT

All of the tales about Zeke do not end with a killing. He often attended sales and auctions around the area, and at one such auction a young man rode up, dismounted, walked up to Zeke, and said, "I am going to kill you, for killing my father." Zeke turned to the young man and said, "Your father and I had trouble, but you haven't done anything to me, and I do not intend to shoot you." The man repeated his threat to Zeke several times, but Zeke refused to listen to him. The young man then mounted his horse and rode away.

## THE SECRET GRAVE

In one improbable story, circulated shortly after Zeke's death, he was said to have been buried with his weapons. As a result, several attempts were made to rob Zeke's grave, and relatives decided to rebury his body in an unmarked location on a bluff overlooking his Illinois River home. Walter Proctor of Proctor, Oklahoma, at the time of this writing owns one of Zeke's .45s and a rifle. Elizabeth Walden recalls attending her grandfather Zeke's funeral when she was eleven and relates that some of his weapons were buried with him. Mrs. Walden further states that an attempt was made to rob Zeke's grave in 1929 but that the grave has never been moved from the Johnson cemetery which was the original Proctor family cemetery.

## ZEKE'S PARTNER'S BANKRUPTCY

John Hargrove was one of the founders and an early merchant of the present city of Siloam Springs, Arkansas. Hargrove and Zeke Proctor were partners for a number of years in the operation of a sawmill that they transported around the area. Both Zeke and Hargrove were lovers of fine horses, and both men maintained and bred blooded horses. Only one reference to a friendship between Belle Starr and Zeke was uncovered by A. D. Lester. The source indicates that Belle sometimes spent the night at Zeke's home when in the area. It stands to reason that they did at least know each other, especially since the cave referred to as the Belle Starr Cave, which Belle often used as a campsite, was only a short distance downriver from Zeke's home. At any rate, Belle Starr was also a breeder of fine horses, and after purchasing a thoroughbred in Kansas, she challenged John Hargrove to a race. One thousand dollars was put up, and Belle told her jockey to win only by a nose, which he did. A few days later Belle again approached Hargrove and challenged him to another race, but this time for five thousand dollars. Hargrove, feeling that his horse, having barely lost the first race, could very well win the next one, put up his five thousand. This time Belle told her jockey to turn her horse loose. Belle's horse ran away from Hargrove's by several lengths, and this financial loss bankrupted Hargrove and dissolved his partnership with Zeke Proctor. Some say Zeke himself lost a large sum on the race.

## THE LITTLE URCHIN

Another ofttold tale describes Zeke as an adopted son of the Proctors. As the story goes, one morning after breakfast the family found a three-year-old Indian boy in their yard, hungry and cold. No one ever knew how he got there or where he came from; they assumed his parents dropped him off on their way through the country. They no longer wanted him because at the age of three he had killed a man. The Proctors kept the boy and named him Zeke. This story is, of course, complete fiction, since Ezekiel was listed as a son of the Proctors on the Cherokee census in Georgia. But its persistance illustrates the imaginative legends that Zeke inspired.

## PROCTOR'S SUPERSTITIONS

All accounts of Zeke's life indicate that he was very superstitious, as most Cherokees were at this time. When a storm cloud would approach his home, he would go to the woodpile, split a log halfway with an ax, then point the ax and log toward the center of the cloud. This procedure was intended to split the cloud and divert the storm. Zeke firmly believed that the Great Spirit looked after him at all times, and throughout his life he appears to have had an uncanny ability to sense and avoid danger. According to legend, Zeke always left a saucer of milk outside his door before retiring for the night. This milk was for the good fairies, and each morning it was always gone.

## ZEKE'S LAST WORDS

Elizabeth Walden related that she was told that Zeke's last words concerned the notorious Wickliffe outlaw gang. As Zeke lay dying of pneumonia, he whispered softly in his last breath, "Feed the boys good." The "boys" were the Wickliffe boys who were hiding in Zeke's barn at the time.

This rare photograph of Belle Starr is believed to have been made in a Fort Smith photographer's shop. (Photograph courtesy Cecil Atchison Collection)

Belle Starr and her outlaw friend Blue Duck. (Photograph courtesy Cecil Atchison Collection)

# Part Two

# NED CHRISTIE

The defiant Ned Christie posed for this photograph in 1889 at the height of his notoriety. The Cherokee outlaw eluded the law for four years before he was trapped by 25 U.S. marshals and an army field cannon. This photograph was obtained from Mrs. William Ellis, wife of one of the marshals who killed Christie. (Photograph courtesy the McKennon Collection)

Ned Christie (right) with his lawyer. This rare photograph, courtesy of Mrs. Nancy Christie Runabout, is believed to have been taken in Tahlequah, Oklahoma. Mrs. Runabout's father, Bill Christie, was Ned's nephew and provided a major portion of the information for this book.

# VIII

## The Man and His Bitterness

At the time that the Proctors were forced to leave their Georgia home for new lands west of Arkansas, Watt Christie, who was born in 1817, was leaving the Carolinas with his family on their long march westward. While the Proctor family followed the Trail of Tears water route, the Christies walked the overland trail to their new home. Arriving in the early 1830s the family settled in the southern portion of the Going Snake District along Bidding Springs Creek. The original home stood directly behind the present general store operated by Mr. and Mrs. Edwin Willis in the small eastern Oklahoma community of Wauhillau. The land is owned today by Mrs. Helen Herrington of Wauhillau.

The name Christie, according to Watt's grandson, Bill Christie, Jr., of Tahlequah, was originally pronounced in Cherokee as Wattie, meaning gourd. Over the years, as the English translation became more predominant, the name Wattie became Christie. Watt Christie took the first part of his original Cherokee name for his first name.

Watt Christie was a master blacksmith by trade, and soon after establishing his home, clearing nearby fields, and planting crops, he built his blacksmith shop near his home. He had brought with him over the trail a few pieces of his most necessary smithing equipment by wagon and he traded for the balance of his needed tools in the nearby Arkansas border towns of Cincinnati and Fort Smith. In that day the blacksmith was in great demand among the Indians, not only for shoeing horses, but also for such necessities as the making and repairing of guns, wagons, cooking utensils, tools, plows, and all types of hardware. Since there were very few skilled blacksmiths in the new Indian nation, Watt Christie's shop soon became the trade center and meeting place for that portion of the Cherokee nation.

Watt was a strikingly handsome Indian and soon collected a harem of the most beautiful Indian maidens in the territory. According to Bill Christie, Jr., Watt had a total of eight wives. The Cherokee wedding laws were quite simple, requiring only mutual consent of the parties in front of witnesses. There seems to have been no limit to the number of wives a man could have as long as he could adequately support each wife and family. Among the Cherokees, a man's wealth and social standing were often judged by the number of wives he had. This would indicate that Watt was an extremely successful blacksmith and farmer.

The original Cherokee tribal wedding ceremony was practiced by many of those who came on the Trail of Tears. The ceremony usually consisted of an all-day party to which everyone wore their gayest apparel. The groom, accompanied by young male associates, feasted at one house, and the bride celebrated with her girl friends at another location. After the feasts, the men sat on one side of the marriage grounds or building and the women on the other. The bride and groom then faced each other some thirty to sixty feet apart. The groom's mother then handed him a leg of venison and a blanket while the bride received from her mother an ear of corn and a blanket. The couple walked toward each other, and when they met, the groom presented his venison to the bride and the bride her ear of corn to the groom. When the blankets united, the marriage rite was completed. The presentation of the venison signified that the groom promised to provide meat for his wife and their children, and with her corn she promised to make the bread. The united blankets signified that they would share the same home.

It is not known whether Watt Christie employed the original ceremony in all of his many marriages. One is struck, however, by the simplicity of the wedding rites among the Cherokees at this time. Lenient marriage laws existed until 1892, at which time the Cherokee council passed more rigid rulings. It is interesting to note, however, that today the state of Oklahoma recognizes a couple as legally married under a common-law arrangement any time they openly hold themselves out to the public as man and wife; but such marriages must be dissolved by legal divorce action. The recognition of common-law marriage no doubt derives from the old Indian customs within the state.

Watt and his various wives were parents of eleven known children. The boys were Ned, Jim, William, Goback, Jack, George, and Lacy. The girls were Katie, who married Colman Dick; Jennie, who married Dave Wolf; Einna, who married a Cherokee named Spade; and Nellie, whose husband, if she had one, is unknown. Watt's grandson Bill, of uncertain age, is living in the Ward Nursing Home of Tahlequah, Oklahoma, at the time of this writing. He provided a great deal of guidance toward a factual account of Ned Christie's life. Although he was only a small boy during his Uncle Ned's period of trouble with the United States government, he vividly recalls his uncle and the details of his many encounters with the United States marshals and bounty hunters. Bill, Jr., recalled that between the years of 1892 and 1895 he often was in or around Ned's home when marshals would attack, and he remembers having to run and dodge to stay out of the line of fire. He still carries a bullet in his hip from a wild shot from Ned's .44. Ned, his brother Lacy, and an Indian named Jacob were drinking and shooting their guns wildly when a bullet accidentally ricocheted and struck young Bill who was playing nearby. The accident left him with a bad limp throughout his life.

On August 8, 1970, Cecil Atchison of Fort Smith, Arkansas, and the writer spent the afternoon with Bill, Jr., in search of facts about Ned Christie and an insight into what this man, many times referred to as Oklahoma's worst outlaw, was really like. Since Bill Christie could not speak English, Bill Bowlin, an eighty-six-year-old Cherokee from Marble City, Oklahoma, and a friend of Christie's went along as an interpreter. Mrs. Nancy Runabout, Bill Christie's daughter, working as a nurse in the Ward Nursing Home, joined the group in the discussion. Many other sources of research have been used in the preparation of Christie's portion of this text, but the writer feels that the information provided by Bill Christie, Jr., the only living person who actually lived in Ned's home during his trouble with the law, to have been invaluable in an effort to separate fact from fiction and establish the deeper causes behind Ned's great bitterness toward the United States.

Ned Christie was born at his father's family home on December, 14, 1852. His boyhood was much like Zeke Proctor's and any other Indian boy of the time. Like Proctor, he was forced to grow up surrounded by renegades who were taking refuge from the law. Over the years young Ned grew to share his father's great bitterness over the loss of their Carolina home and their tribe's mistreatment on the Trail of Tears. He too found it necessary to learn to handle a gun at a very early age. Watt was one of the region's best blacksmiths for handling and repairing firearms, and Ned soon learned his father's skills. Before he was ten years of age Ned was ranked as one of the best marksmen in the Cherokee nation, and his elders marveled at the lad's ability.

Ned had a natural agility with and appreciation for all kinds of weapons at an early age, and his gunsmithing skill came into great demand throughout the Cherokee nation. When Watt Christie returned home after his service in the Civil War, he gave Ned his two .44 × .40 cap-and-ball pistols. Ned went to work immediately in his dad's shop and converted the pistols from cap-and-ball to shell-percussion five-shot pistols. Although Ned had many, many weapons throughout his life, the original .44s he got from his father were to remain his favorite weapons, and he had them both in his hands when he died many years later.

Watt Christie was highly respected throughout the Indian nation, and he served in many positions within the Cherokee government during his lifetime. His popular blacksmith shop was the scene of many meetings and discussions relating to tribal government and United States interference within their nation. Thus, Ned grew up with a thorough knowledge of the Cherokee government, its laws, and problems with the federal government. Most of Ned's education derived from these shop sessions, for he had little if any formal education. As he grew to manhood he came to share his father's strong belief in a free Cherokee nation and at the same time to hate anyone who tried to destroy the principles in which his father and the Keetoowa Society believed.

No doubt it was through the Keetoowa Society that the Proctors and the Christies became acquainted. Zeke Proctor and his family were also like the Christies in strongly advocating Cherokee national independence. Bill Christie, Jr., in his interview with the writer, stated, "Ned Christie and Zeke Proctor were great friends." Bill further stated that Zeke frequented the Christie blacksmith shop and often called on Ned for his skill in gunsmithing. Ned was some twenty-one years younger than Zeke, but since they lived only some thirty miles apart and both families were active in government and Keetoowa matters, it is the writer's opinion that they most likely were friends. The writer has not found, however, any mention of Proctor and Christie being friends in any other interview or research material used. Therefore, it is only assumed that whatever friendship or relationship there was between the Proctor and Christie families was, at the most, a casual one.

Bill Christie, Jr., also recalled that Watt and Ned both

attended Proctor's trial at the Whitmire schoolhouse. Being strong supporters of the Keetoowa Society and the Proctor cause, the Christies supported the Proctor faction in the battle that erupted when Marshal Owens' posse disrupted the trial proceedings. During the short period between Proctor's trial and his treaty with the United States, Proctor and some fifty supporters from the Pin Indian Organization were on the scout to prevent any further action from Fort Smith's federal court. It is not known whether Ned or his father, Watt, rode with this group protecting Proctor. The Proctor case did, however, greatly contribute to Ned Christie's growing bitterness against the United States government.

Resembling his father, Ned grew to be an extremely handsome man. He stood six feet, four inches in height and carried himself straight and tall. He walked with a proud air and wore his black hair to his shoulders. Like Zeke Proctor, Ned Christie also had an almost supernatural ability to sense danger and often amazed those around him with this sixth sense he seemed to possess. It was said that during his battles with United States authorities in later years, he would often predict attacks a few hours before marshals arrived and prepare for them while they were still many miles away.

As a result of the exceptional quality and skill father and son offered, the blacksmith and gunsmith shop grew even more rapidly. Also, Ned's handsome appearance made him attractive to the most beautiful of eligible Cherokee maidens. Bill Christie, Jr., described his Uncle Ned as a great lover who "slept with a different wife almost every night." The exact number of wives he had is not known, but as wives went, Ned Christie, like his father, was considered to be a quite wealthy Cherokee. No doubt Ned had several children, but Bill Christie, Jr., stated that he knew of only one son, Arch Christie. There is a belief drawn from cemetery recordings that Ned might have had a daughter named Jennie. It is the writer's opinion, however, that the Jennie referred to in these records was actually Ned's sister. It should be mentioned that there were several Christie families living in the Cherokee nation at this time, who were of no relation to Ned or his family. The community of Christie, Oklahoma, was named after another Christie family and not the Ned or Watt families. Although there were most likely other children from Ned's many wife relationships, it appears from all research that Arch Christie was the only child with whom he had a close father-and-son relationship.

Ned, seasoned from early childhood by his father and the discussions around his shop, grew to be an even more belligerent speaker against federal interference within their nation as time went by. Ned's leadership ability and his outspoken patriotism to the Cherokee nation and its principles soon got him elected to a position within the Cherokee council, similar to that of a United States senator.

There were three branches of government within the Cherokee nation, the legislative, or the National Council; the executive, or the National Committee; and the judicial. The executive branch was later referred to as the Senate. The Senate consisted of two members from each district of the Cherokee nation, and the National Council consisted of three members from each district. Ned represented the Going Snake District in 1885, along, with David Muskrat and Daniel Redbird. The system greatly resembled that of the United States. The Senate proposed and drafted bills. Once bills were proposed, the National Council reviewed them, and then either passed them along to the tribal chief for signing or returned them to the Senate for further review. The chief could return any proposal to the National Council or could sign them into law. Ned Christie's service in his government's legislature, his masterful skill as a gunsmith, and his loyalty and enthusiasm toward the building of a Cherokee nation free of outside interference gained him great popularity and respect throughout the Cherokee nation.

Railroads were being built through Indian Territory, bringing many white traders and merchants who became adopted citizens of the Cherokee nation. More and more white citizens were found settling on rich farmlands within the nation. The Cherokee treaties provided that the Cherokee government had authority of law over any adopted citizen of their nation as well as over their Indian citizens. The Cherokees' authority over any United States citizen who might be in their nation, however, was questionable, since it was sometimes hard to distinguish between adopted whites and those who were only visitors. The Cherokee government inflicted little law enforcement on the whites in their nation, because they feared reprisals from United States authorities. The increasing settlement of Cherokee lands by white citizens of the United States was looked upon by Christie and the Keetoowa Society as infringement on the tribe's original treaty rights. Ned's bitterness over the situation grew to almost a point of rage, and through his government position and society leadership, he gained many supporters. Also, around 1885 Americans began talking about statehood for Oklahoma, and these whites living within the Indian nation were no doubt also promoting statehood. It is generally believed that this situation contributed greatly in changing Ned Christie's character and personality from that of the beloved, jovial, and peaceful citizen to a belligerent outlaw.

Deputy U.S. Marshal Dan Maples of Bentonville, Arkansas. He was one of the 65 lawmen killed in action while policing Indian Territory. Ned Christie was accused of killing Maples in Tahlequah, Indian Territory, on May 4, 1887. The above photograph belongs to Mrs. Beatrice Maples Jones of Bentonville, granddaughter of Dan Maples. Mrs. Jones's grandmother, Maples' wife, lived with Mrs. Jones until her death, and it is from her actual account that most of the information regarding her husband's slaying was taken. (Photograph courtesy Mrs. Beatrice Maples Jones)

Sam Maples, son of Deputy U.S. Marshal Dan Maples. Ned Christie was accused of killing Dan Maples, and revenge for his father's death haunted young Sam Maples for five years. Rushing to the scene where Christie had fallen, Maples emptied his two pistols into the body. Sam Maples never returned to his native Bentonville, Arkansas, after Christie's death. He went immediately to California and then became a rancher in Canada. A few years later he froze to death in a Canadian "Black Blizzard" near his home. (Photo courtesy Mrs. Beatrice Maples Jones)

The body of Ned Christie shortly after he was killed by twenty-five deputy U.S. marshals. Christie's body was strapped to boards taken from his cabin door. The body was propped up on the steps of Parker's court in Fort Smith for this photograph. Before the picture was taken, Deputy Marshal Hugh Harp laid his rifle in Christie's hands because he thought any picture of the desperate outlaw should depict him holding a weapon. (Photograph courtesy Cecil Atchison Collection)

The rock fort that Ned Christie and his followers held atop a mountain near his home was virtually impregnable, and Christie and his band of followers held off several posses from here while his log fort was being completed a mile away. The mountain became known as Ned Fort Mountain, and it is so called today. (Photograph by Phillip Steele)

# IX

## *The Murder of*
## *Deputy Marshal Maples*

Although Christie had grown increasingly bitter in his concern for total Cherokee independence, his actions up until May 4, 1887, consisted only of occasional angry speeches against the United States. Until this date he had been accused of no crime and was respected throughout the Cherokee nation. On the night of May 4, however, Christie was accused of the murder of Daniel Maples, deputy United States marshal at Bentonville, Arkansas. The circumstances surrounding his accusation greatly resembled those Zeke Proctor had faced fifteen years earlier. This night was the turning point in Ned's life and personality, and subsequent developments set off the beginning of his personal war with the United States that was to last nearly five years.

Daniel Maples was serving as deputy marshal in the Benton County, Arkansas, district for Judge Isaac C. Parker's federal court at Fort Smith. Residing in Bentonville, the county seat, with his wife Maletha and children Sam, Arch, George, Leona, Pearl, and Bert, he and his family had become highly regarded throughout the region. Maples had virtually done away with crime in his area, and for this the citizens of Bentonville and Benton County had good reason to greatly admire him.

Mrs. Beatrice Maples Jones of Bentonville, Arkansas, is the granddaughter of Dan Maples, her father being George

Maples, Dan's youngest son. Mrs. Jones's grandmother, Maletha Maples, lived with her until her death December 17, 1929. Mrs. Maples had learned the facts of her husband's slaying from her son Sam and from Mack Peel and George Jefferson, all of whom had accompanied him to Tahlequah, Indian Territory, on May 2, 1887. This account and several contemporary newspaper clippings in Mrs. Jones's possession present a case that contradicts to some degree the accounts given by most previous writers concerning Dan Maples' death. Although several other descriptions have been studied in the preparation of this text, the writer has chosen to use the account Mrs. Jones received directly from Mrs. Dan Maples and the newspaper articles that appeared at the time of the murder to be the most accurate.

On Monday, May 2, 1887, Deputy Marshal Dan Maples received orders from Marshal John Carroll in Fort Smith to take a posse to Tahlequah, search out and apprehend the noted desperado Bill Pigeon, and bring him to Fort Smith to stand trial for many crimes charged against him. Early on this date Dan, his sixteen-year-old son Sam, Mack Peel, George Jefferson, and a Bentonville youth hired as a cook, left on their two-day journey to Tahlequah. Mrs. Maples often told the story of trying to stop her husband from going on this particular mission. She had never interfered with his duties, but as he was saddling his horse on this particular morning a strange thing happened. A large black bird flew down and landed on Dan Maples' shoulder, and Mrs. Maples, who was watching, considered this to be a bad omen. She feared death for her husband and tried, in vain, to persuade him not to go.

Arriving in Tahlequah early on the morning of Wednesday, May 4, 1887, the five men quickly set up camp along Tahlequah Creek on the outskirts of this bustling community that was the capital of the Cherokee nation and a busy trade center. Maples and George Jefferson then left the others in camp and went into the city to inquire around town as to the whereabouts of Pigeon and to do some trading. At dusk that day they were returning to camp, and just as they were crossing the creek on a footlog, scarcely one hundred yards from camp, Jefferson saw the flash of a shiny revolver from behind a tree. He yelled at Maples to watch out just as the assassin emptied the gun into Maples. Jefferson often mentioned that he was in front of Maples standing upright, an easy target in the open, but was not struck by any of the two full chambers the gunman fired. Maples was struck by the first bullet, but as he fell managed to draw his gun and fire four rounds at his attacker. Hearing the shots, Sam Maples, Mack Peel, and the cook grabbed their weapons in camp and ran to the scene. The slayer had disappeared into the woods, however, by the time they arrived. Dan Maples had been shot several times but was still alive. He was taken to a Tahlequah residence where he received the best care possible by one of the citizens who had some experience at medical practice. Maples lived through the night and died early on the morning of Thursday, May 5, 1887.

Returning with the body, Sam Maples, George Jefferson, Mack Peel, and the cook passed through Fayetteville, Arkansas, on their way to Bentonville on Friday, May 6. The citizens of Fayetteville, who had heard of Maples' death and were enraged by it, met the party and requested a full report of how it happened. The account these men gave the citizens of Fayetteville was reported in the Fayetteville newspaper. Mrs. Beatrice Maples Jones still has a copy of this article and states that her grandmother, Mrs. Dan Maples, George Jefferson, and Mack Peel, all of whom lived in Bentonville for many years afterward, agreed with the reporter's description of the murder.

Most of the county's citizens were in Bentonville to express their sympathy and great disgust over the bloody slaying of their revered citizen. One newspaper account stated, "no man had more or warmer friends than did Dan Maples." The aroused people demanded that Fort Smith's federal court take immediate action in running down and apprehending Maples' assassin. Governor Simon P. Hughes of Arkansas offered a reward of $1,500 for the capture of the slayer, dead or alive. Chief Bushyhead, then chief of the Cherokee nation, also arranged for a reward and pledged his government's support in tracking down the murderer. This reward and Cherokee support is described in an article that appeared in the Tahlequah *Democrat* a few days after Maples' murder:

> At the meeting of the citizens of Tahlequah regarding the recent shooting of U.S. deputy marshal Dan Maples the following resolutions were passed. Resolve that we the undersigned citizens of Tahlequah deeply deplore the recent murder in our midst and our heartfelt sympathy is hereby extended to his friends and loved ones at home in the great loss they have sustained. Resolve further that we bitterly condemn and abhor the commission of so terrible and unusual a crime within our midst and we ask the principle chief to use what means he has in his power to arrest the guilty party and deliver him to the proper authority in conformity with the intercourse laws of the United States which by treaty are made obligatory on us.

> The resolutions were signed by a great many. Chief Bushyhead started the list with his signature and will offer a reward of $300 for the arrest of the slayer and besides this the citizens are making up a private reward. There are said to be strong indications that a clue had been hit upon. The citizens will do all in their power to catch and bring to trial this slayer.

Ned Christie had left his home early on May 4 for Tahlequah and a session of the Senate to begin Thursday, May 5. That evening Ned and a friend, John Parris, went to the home of Jennie Schell for whiskey. Her home was a popular place in Tahlequah and provided not only whiskey but also women and other entertainment for her guests. Jennie's house was near the scene of the Maples killing, and the next morning the Cherokee Light Horse police questioned her about the crime. She told them that Ned Christie and John Parris, both very drunk, had left her house shortly before the shooting.

Parris was quickly found and arrested for Maples' murder. As Christie was leaving his hotel for the Senate session, he was approached by one of his friends in the legislature and told about the accusations against him. Parris, upon arrest, had told the authorities that Ned Christie, not he, had fired the gun that killed Maples. Christie wanted to go at once to the jail and tell them that Parris was lying and that he knew nothing of the crime, but his friend convinced him that he should run and hide until he could establish an alibi or other proof of his innocence. The fact that he was now a hunted man with a reward on his head, dead or alive, for a crime he swore he didn't commit greatly enraged Ned Christie. He somehow slipped out of town undetected by the authorities. He again thought of going directly to Fort Smith and declaring his innocence, but he knew that it was only his word against that of Parris with no other witness or means to establish his innocence. Without such proof and with tremendous pressure on the court by Arkansas citizens to find and hang the slayer of Maples, he knew he would surely hang if he went to Fort Smith. In the hope of establishing his willingness to cooperate with the authorities to prove his innocence, Ned sent a messenger to Judge Parker stating he was innocent and requesting the right of bail to give him and authorities time to find the real killer. Since Maples was one of some sixty-five United States marshals who had been slain in the region, Parker was by no means in a position to grant bail to Ned Christie. Upon the messenger's return, Ned surrounded himself with an army of men, mostly members of the Keetoowa Society, and set up a heavily armed barricade around his home. Sentries were posted for miles around to warn him of approaching trouble, and Ned's fight for survival and his personal war against the United States began.

From the time of Ned Christie's death, which was to occur four years later, until 1922 it was generally believed that he was the slayer of Dan Maples, although he continually denied any knowledge of the crime. It was not until thirty years after Ned's death that a witness to the murder came forward and cleared Christie of the crime. The account this witness gave was reported in a Tulsa, Oklahoma, newspaper editorial in 1992 headlined, MURDER OF U.S. MARSHAL CLEARED 30 YEARS LATER.

The article, written by Fred E. Sutton, if factual, would prove a great source of embarrassment to all of the law authorities who so diligently battled Christie for four long years and finally succeeded in killing him. For some reason all of the past writers on Christie were either unaware of this witness to the Maples murder and the 1922 editorial or did not feel it to be worthy of mention. This writer feels, however, that this account by a witness to the murder is most probably factual since the witness had nothing to gain by coming forward at so late a date other than to derive relief for a guilty conscience.

The editorial was based on the story given Mr. Sutton by Dick Humphrey, a Negro blacksmith in Tahlequah at the time of Maples' death. Humphrey stated he was on his way to Jennie Schell's house for his customary drink of whiskey after a hard day's work when he spotted Bud Trainor taking a coat off Ned Christie, who was lying in the grass in a drunken stupor. Suspecting foul play, Humphrey stated, he then hid behind a large tree and waited to see what was going to happen.

Humphrey further stated that earlier in the day Dan Maples had gone into the store and post office operated by Jim Stapler and told him that he wanted to use his telephone—which was the only one in Tahlequah—after the store closed. A man by the name of Wynn was shopping in the store and overheard Maples' conversation with Stapler. Wynn then waited until Stapler closed the store and watched for Maples to return. Wynn then hid himself outside a rear window and listened as Maples called Marshal Carroll in Fort Smith. He overheard Maples tell headquarters that he wanted warrants issued for Jennie Schell and Mandy Sprigston because they were selling illegal whiskey. Wynn then ran to the Triplett home in Tahlequah where a dance was in progress. Laughter and a hot Arkansas fiddle could be heard coming from the house. A large crowd was at the dance, and most of the men were drinking whiskey they had obtained from Jennie Schell. Soon Bud Trainor came out and talked a few minutes with John Parris. Trainor checked his two .45s and then ran for the Tahlequah Creek where he found Christie lying in the grass drunk.

Humphrey waited in the dark, and soon Dan Maples came along apparently on his way to arrest Jennie Schell. As Maples crossed the footlog leading to her house, Humphrey saw Bud Trainor empty his two guns into Maples and flee into the darkness. Humphrey said that Maples fired four shots at Trainor as he fell.

The next morning Christie awoke from his drunken slumber and went into town with no knowledge of the Maples slaying or of the accusation against him. The rest of the Humphrey story was like the first account. Humphrey stated that he did not come forward because he knew Trainor had many friends; he was afraid no one would believe him and he would be killed. A few years later Trainor was shot and killed, and Humphrey again debated on coming forward, but he feared the many outlaw friends Trainor had. Humphrey, therefore, carried the eyewitness account of the crime with him until his old age in 1922 at which time he gave the account to the Tulsa newspaper reporter.

George Jefferson of Bentonville, Arkansas, stated throughout his lifetime that he never saw the figure who fired the gun. Just why John Parris told authorities he saw Christie kill Maples is not known. It can only be surmised that Parris was afraid he would hang for the murder if he didn't come up with a story. Humphrey's story cannot be irrevocably proved, of course; but Christie denied his guilt to the last and in his determination to survive became an outlaw.

# X

## Christie's Four Long Years of War

It was shortly after Zeke Proctor had been granted amnesty by the United States that Judge Isaac C. Parker was appointed to the bench of Fort Smith's federal court on March 11, 1875, by President Ulysses S. Grant. Until this time, crime along Arkansas' western border had grown continuously worse, and most of the nation's outlaws and killers were using the Indian nation as a refuge from the law. Parker was assigned the tremendous duty of restoring law along the Arkansas border and throughout the Indian nation. He, who was to go down in history as the "hanging judge," as a result of some seventy-nine men hanged on his gallows, was determined to bring law and order to the region at any cost. Along with Marshal John Carroll, who served the court from 1885 to 1889, and Marshal Jacob Yoes, who served from 1889 to 1893, Parker succeeded in bringing many criminals to justice, and the great fear of Parker and his marshals brought some semblance of peace throughout the formerly lawless region.

Parker and his men were justly proud of the progress their court had made, and the killing of Dan Maples, one of the best deputy marshals, brought them to immediate action and the hope that Christie could be apprehended quickly. They wanted no major outbreak of crime which would impede the court's progress. The writer is greatly indebted to Cecil Atchison of Fort Smith, Arkansas, for providing much

of the information and many details of the four years that
followed Dan Maples' death. Atchison, who at the time of
this writing owns most of the display pieces in Parker's Court
Museum at Fort Smith, has spent a lifetime researching and
collecting historical data on Parker's court, Arkansas border
history, and Indian nation history. During his lifetime he has
known many deputy United States marshals who worked for
Parker. In interviews with Deputy Marshal Spunky Taylor,
Harp, and others, Atchison recorded recollections of the
many battles the marshals had with Christie. It is from these
interviews, the writer's interviews with Bill Christie, who
actually lived with or near his Uncle Ned during these years,
and from references to the publication of the original *Hell on
the Border* by Frank L. Van Eaton, that the details of
Christie's four years under siege are taken.

Arriving at his home some twelve miles east of Tahlequah, Ned Christie told his wife and his son Arch of the
murder accusation against him. Ned immediately got his .44
Colt revolvers down from the cupboard and began cleaning
them after which he carefully loaded them both and rode to
the home of Eli Wilson who lived on a nearby farm. He had
been wanting Wilson's new Winchester Model 73 (.44 × .40
caliber) for some time, and after he related his predicament,
Wilson sold him his new rifle. Christie then carefully stocked
his cabin with ammunition and laid out his weapons for easy
access around the house. He then called many of his friends
together to discuss his situation and to outline a plan of
defense. From these friends, mostly members of the Keetoowa Society, Christie established a small army. Sentries
were posted at several miles' distance around his home to
report immediately any approaching lawmen or bounty
hunters. During the months that followed, many attempts
were made by some of Parker's best marshals to capture
Christie, but none was successful in routing him from his
heavily guarded stronghold. The rolling hills and dense for-
est surrounding Christie's home gave him every advantage.

He had become something of a hero to his followers, and as time passed, his army of supporters grew to such an extent that it was suicidal for anyone to attempt to capture Christie.

In 1889 Heck Thomas, who had gained a widespread reputation as a lawman for running down the notorious train robber Sam Bass in Texas, joined Parker's force. He immediately began making plans to capture Christie. Thomas secured Deputy U.S. Marshal L. P. Isbel, a seasoned veteran from Vinita, as a guide to the territory surrounding Christie's home. In the hope of avoiding the attention of Christie's sentries, Thomas and Isbel and three possemen approached Christie's home at night from five different directions. Near daybreak each one succeeded in arriving undetected at their planned meeting place near the house. As the men tied their horses and began creeping forward, Ned's dogs began barking. Ned awakened, grabbed his pistols and rifle, and rushed up to the loft where he kicked open a shutter and sent forth a barrage of fire that sent the men scurrying for cover. As Ned fired repeatedly, his wife and son kept reloading his weapons. The heavy fire forced the men to a retreat where they planned their next move. Christie's gunshop was near his home, and Thomas correctly suspected that Christie highly valued his smithing shop and its many tools. If the gunshop could be set on fire, Christie would surely come out and attempt to save it.

Thomas crawled up to the shop, piled kindling against it, and set it on fire as Deputy Marshal Isbel covered his actions. Isbel, who was firing from behind a large tree, exposed his right shoulder, and Christie instantly sent a bullet smashing into it. Thomas pulled Isbel to safety and fixed a crude bandage to the wound that was to paralyze Isbel's arm for life and thus end his career as a deputy U.S. marshal. At this point, Christie's wife ran from the house. The flames from the gunshop had now reached the woods. Thinking the figure was Christie, Thomas raised and fired at the fleeing woman. As he fired, another shot grazed Thomas' head.

Christie then leaped from the burning house and followed his son into the woods. Thomas fired again, and just as Christie reached the brush the deputy saw him grab his head and fall.

With Isbel's wound bleeding profusely, Thomas had no recourse but to retreat at once to get medical aid. Leaving Isbel with one of the posse, Thomas and the two other men searched the wooded area for Christie. Finding no sign of him, the party then returned to Fort Smith. Arch Christie had received a wound in the chest and Ned a bullet in the right temple. Christie's friends, who had been lurking in the woods, pulled Ned and Arch to safety as they entered the area. Arch Christie's lung had been punctured, but he soon recovered. Ned's wound was even more serious. The bullet from Thomas' gun had entered his right temple and lodged in his skull. It blinded his right eye and smashed the bone structure in his nose. After several months Christie's wound healed, but the deep scar on his face and his sightless right eye had greatly disfigured his formerly handsome face. He had been justly proud of his appearance, and this disfigurement turned his already belligerent personality into one of great viciousness. He swore an oath never to speak the English language again and never to leave his beloved hills of the Cherokee nation.

For Ned's recuperation from his wound, his friends constructed a wooden shelter within a natural rock-wall encirclement on the top of a hill a short distance from his homesite. This natural rock fort offered a view for many miles in all directions, and the large rock wall made it virtually impregnable. The structure was loaded with enough ammunition to hold out for weeks. Food, water, and other necessary provisions were also carefully stored in sufficient supply to sustain Christie and his men for long periods of time.

Since the famous Heck Thomas had not been successful and since word of Christie's mountaintop arsenal had spread throughout the region, no one felt they were strong enough to try to take him. Most of the marshals believed that it would require a large regiment of United States militia to stand up to Christie and the powerful defense surrounding him.

Left in peace for several months, Ned decided to rebuild his burned out home and shop. This time he would build not only adequate living quarters for his family, but also a permanent fort that would provide him with maximum security. There was an excellent spring in a little valley near his original house. This spring, which still flows today, is called Christie Springs. Instead of rebuilding his new home on his old homesite, he decided to build on the opposite side of the valley, eastward, and directly above the spring.

Christie obtained a steam engine which he used to power a sawmill for construction of his new home and fort. The house was a two-story structure with walls of two-log thickness and filled between with sand. The upstairs area had no windows, only slits through which rifles could be fired, offering maximum protection. The inside walls were lined with oak two-by-fours for further bulletproofing. Like the mountaintop fort, his new home was heavily armed and supplied to withstand long periods of battle.

Shortly after Ned Christie completed his new fort in 1891, Dave Rusk, another deputy marshal who had earned a reputation as a lawman, decided to try his luck at capturing the dreaded outlaw whom no one had been able to match. Rusk, having served as captain of Company A, First Battalion of The Missouri Calvary, CSA, during the Civil War, knew the Cherokee nation well. Before becoming a lawman he was an exhibition pistol shooter with a circus and was one of the best marksmen ever to be on Parker's force. Rusk was sworn in as a deputy marshal at Fort Smith in 1875.

In 1891 Rusk organized a posse made up mostly of Cherokees who were not sympathetic to the Christie faction. They surrounded the new fort, and four of their number were wounded in the first volley of fire from Christie. Rusk quickly called off the fight, but over the next year, he made several other attempts to slip up on Christie. His last attack resulted in a bullet hole through his large black stetson, and once more the project was temporarily abandoned.

Christie was well aware that Deputy Marshal Rusk was the one who had been dogging him for many months. Rusk, while serving as deputy, had also been operating several business enterprises around the territory. He erected the first brick building to house a hotel in the border city of Siloam Springs, Arkansas. Shortly before his first attempt to capture Christie, Rusk had opened a general merchandise store in the community of Oaks, some twenty miles north of Tahlequah in the Cherokee nation, and he had moved his family to Oaks. Fearing reprisal from a band of outlaws known as the Cabin Gang, which surrounded Christie and his fort, Rusk decided to move his family to Joplin, Missouri, for safety. While he was away Christie and his followers struck. The gang shot up the store, destroyed the merchandise, and burned the building. A young Indian clerk named William Israel had been left to mind the store. Finding one of their own tribesmen working for a white man, and especially a deputy United States marshal who was trying to capture Christie, the gang took Israel, poured a large amount of whiskey down his throat, then tarred and feathered him.

This was Christie's first counterattack against his enemies. Until this time, he had fought back only when his home was attacked. After destroying the Rusk store, the gang was accused of making many similar attacks on trading posts and stores operated by white settlers throughout the region. However, there were many outlaw bands operating in the region at the time, and Christie was identified only as participating in the Rusk store raid. Fear of Christie had grown to such a point by this time that he was blamed for practically all acts of violence within the territory, and many outlaw gangs used the opportunity to deal their violence and go unidentified.

U.S. Deputy Marshal Hugh Harp in later years. Harp was present when Christie's body was brought in and displayed on the steps of Fort Smith's federal court. Cecil Atchison, from whom a major portion of the information was obtained in the preparation of this text, received much of his knowledge regarding Christie and his capture from an interview with Deputy Harp. (Photograph courtesy Cecil Atchison Collection)

John R. Tolbert, Paden Tolbert's brother, and a member of the posse that killed Ned Christie. Deputy Marshal John Tolbert organized the Fort Smith selected marshals for his brother Paden's posse. John then met Paden and his men at the Fort Smith railroad depot for their trip to West Fork, Arkansas. (Photograph courtesy Cecil Atchison Collection)

·Deputy U.S. Marshal Heck Thomas, one of the most famous of all frontier lawmen. He served as a Texas ranger and as a deputy marshal for Fort Smith's federal court. He killed eleven desperate outlaws during his lifetime, including the notorius Bill Doolin, who eluded law authorities for a number of years. Thomas served as a lawman all of his adult life and died in Lawton, Oklahoma, in 1912. Heck Thomas tried several times to capture Ned Christie. (Photograph courtesy ·Cecil Atchison Collection)

# XI

## *The Final Siege*

      Ned Christie had succeeded in overpowering the best of Judge Parker's men for four hard years and had proved to be a great source of embarrassment for Parker. The Fort Smith court was receiving tremendous pressure from Washington to bring Christie and the Cabin Gang to justice. The region's citizens were also growing tired of living in constant fear of Christie and his followers and were demanding that the Fort Smith court somehow put a stop to him and his growing outlaw support.

      Judge Parker and United States Marshal Jacob Yoes began making plans for one final attempt to capture Christie. Once more, the best of Parker's marshals were given the assignment of bringing the Indian in at any cost. On October 11, 1892, a posse surrounded Christie's fort. The party consisted of Deputy Marshals Dave Rusk, Charlie Copeland, Milo Creekmore, Joe Bower, D. C. Dye, and John Fields. As usual, Christie had been alerted and was ready for his attackers. Before a shot was fired, Dave Rusk called out to Christie requesting him to surrender and telling him that this time they were prepared to fight to their death. Christie answered with the gobbling sound of the Cherokee death cry and sent forth a volley of fire that wounded Fields and Bowers badly. The posse was retreating to reorganize when several women and children ran from Christie's fort. The posse learned from the women that Christie had three companions with him. Surveying the surroundings for possible strategy, they spotted a farm wagon. Pulling the wagon out of the line of fire they filled it with brush and kindling from Christie's nearby sawmill and set the wagon on fire. It was placed in a position whereby it could easily be rolled on smooth ground to the fort. Several men then pushed the flaming wagon into the side of the fort under a heavy cover of fire by marshals on the opposite side of the building. The wagon hit the side of the fort and fell apart, quickly burning out and doing little damage to Christie's stronghold.

Charlie Copeland then tied together several sticks of dynamite and affixed a long fuse. With a mighty effort the bomb was hurled across the large clearing surrounding the fort and struck a wall of the fort. The impact knocked the fuse loose and the dynamite had no effect.

Once more retreating, the lawmen had a quick consultation and then sent Deputy Creekmore on his way to Tahlequah to seek assistance. At Tahlequah, Creekmore wired Marshal Yoes in Fort Smith: "SEND DEPUTIES TO NED CHRISTIES AT ONCE. WE HAVE SURROUNDED HIM BUT NEED MORE MEN. BOWERS AND FIELDS ARE SHOT AND WILL DIE."

Marshal Yoes answered the wire a few hours later: "HAVE WIRED EVERYWHERE FOR DEPUTIES. YOU WILL HAVE LOTS OF HELP TONIGHT. HOLD FORT BY ALL MEANS AND GET THEM THIS TIME."

That night a total of thirty men had surrounded the fort, but the increased number of men proved to be of little assistance. Christie and his companions, Bear Paw, Walkabout, and Peek Above carefully secured all sides of the fort, and it was sure death for any posseman to venture into the clearing around the fort. Several hours of heavy fire resulted in little if any damage to the fort, and Christie's ammunition supply seemed to be limitless. Tired, out of ammunition, and realizing they were making no progress in this attempt at capturing Christie, the posse returned to Fort Smith.

Shortly after they returned and Copeland made a full report of the situation, Marshal Yoes summoned Paden Tolbert to his office. Yoes selected Tolbert to put together a contingent of the best lawmen in the country to make still another attempt at ridding the region of this desperate killer. The morning was spent in discussing detailed plans for this final siege.

Leaving Yoes's office, Tolbert set out to carefully select the group of men who were to comprise this mighty force. Tolbert first selected Deputy Wess Bowman, and the two men then went by train to Clarksville, Arkansas, to select other needed men. Tolbert had requested Sheriff John Bowers to call the men he had selected to a night meeting in the Clarksville courthouse. The meeting was held at night to avoid any publicity and chance of alerting Christie's followers to the recruitment of another posse. As night fell all of the men selected had gathered for the important meeting. Tolbert told the group of the job for which they had been personally selected and of the plan of attack Marshal Yoes, Judge Parker, and he had discussed. After the long speech and a question-and-answer session, Tolbert took out his note pad and began recording the names of those who would join the posse. As Tolbert had expected, each man selected agreed to go, and Sheriff Bowers then handed out weapons and ammunition to the party consisting of Frank Sarber, Tol Blackard, Oscar Blackard, and Vent Gray. Frank (Becky) Polk, a tall black man, had been selected to cook for the party. Polk had served with Tolbert on many such missions and was not only an excellent cook but also could handle weapons as well as any man.

The next morning the men boarded the train for Fort Smith where they were to meet John Tolbert, Paden's brother, and those lawmen from the Fort Smith area selected to accompany the group. John Tolbert's party consisted of Bill Ellis of Hartshorne, Indian Territory; E. B. Ratterree and I. T. Ratterree of Poteau, Indian Territory; Harry Clayland, and G. S. White. Clayland at age seventeen was the youngest member of the group.

G. S. White had been assigned to secure the posse's supplies. Shortly after the Clarksville group arrived, the men helped White load the supplies and ammunition onto the train the party was to take to West Fork, Arkansas, some sixty miles north of Forth Smith. In West Fork they were to rendezvous with another group of deputies selected from the northwest Arkansas region and lay out final plans for taking Christie.

Deputy Marshal Gus York of West Fork met the train with a wagon and team of strong mules to haul the ammunition and supplies. Three days earlier G. S. White had located a field cannon at a blacksmith shop in Coffeeville, Kansas. The cannon and forty rounds of shells were shipped down to West Fork, where York had arranged to unload and hold them for the posse's arrival. While the men loaded the cannon, ammunition, several boxes of dynamite, black powder, and rifles onto the wagon, Becky Polk went into the little town to purchase the necessary food supplies.

Learning of the posse's plans, Dan Maples' son Sam met the group in West Fork. George Jefferson and Mack Peel, who also had been in Maples' party when he was killed, had accompanied young Maples from Bentonville and requested permission from Paden Tolbert to join the group. Tolbert was somewhat reluctant to let Maples join. The boy had sworn to someday kill his father's murderer, and Tolbert was afraid he might take a foolish chance to satisfy his personal hatred toward Christie. After being assured by Jefferson and Peel that the youth was capable of handling weapons well and would obey orders, Sam Maples was accepted. Two other men, Mills and Birkett, also met the group. Both were noted lawmen and had served with Tolbert in several manhunts. Mills was a blacksmith from Sulphur City, Arkansas, and Birkett was a former sheriff of Washington County, Arkansas.

After the swearing in of the welcome additions to the posse, all of the men helped load the heavy cannon onto the wagon. The thick barrel was four feet in length and was mounted on a heavy oak carriage. There was a screw wheel to adjust elevation of the barrel but no means of adjustment from side to side other than manually moving the heavy carriage. There were no wheels on the oak frame. Bullet-wedged projectiles had been selected over the cannon balls with the hope that the wedged bullets would split and tear the heavy log walls of Christie's fort.

As soon as Becky returned with the food supplies, the men mounted horses that York had provided and set out on their mission. Deputy York had been assigned to other important business and could not accompany the party.

The posse spent their first night at J. S. Summers' store near the border of Indian Territory. In later years the small community of Summers, Arkansas, grew up around this store. Cherokee Sheriff Ben Knight, who did not sympathize with the Christie cause, had been selected as a guide for the group, and he met the party at Summers' store. Charlie Copeland and Heck Bruner, seasoned lawmen from nearby Siloam Springs who also had been selected as possemen, joined the party at Summers.

The next morning, November 1, 1892, the party thanked the host for a hospitable night's lodging and headed into Indian Territory. Tolbert had planned for the posse to arrive at Christie's fort shortly after sundown of that day. Near Barron Fork, Indian Territory, they stopped for a brief rest and met two more deputy marshals who had been requested by Tolbert to join their party at this point. Deputy Bill Smith, half Cherokee, and Deputy Tom Johnson were noted United States marshals, and each had brought in some of the .erritory's worst outlaws over their years of service.

As the sun lowered in the sky on the brisk fall day, Ben Knight went to the front of the column and turned off the main road, heading the posse onto a narrow trail that wound through the heavily forested region. The men now rode single-file with the wagon bringing up the rear. They were instructed to not talk and to ride as quietly as possible. Shortly after dark, Knight halted the group just over a ridge from Christie's lair, and the riders tied their horses and set up camp.

Deputy Marshal Rusk had been instructed to meet the party at this campsite, and upon his arrival the party consisted of twenty-five of the most capable lawmen in frontier history.

While Becky prepared their evening meal, which consisted of canned sardines and crackers since they didn't want to build a fire, Rusk gave a detailed description of the Christie fort and the topography surrounding it. He also strongly emphasized the importance of maintaining cover at all times and warned the men of Christie's deadly and uncanny accuracy with a rifle.

The men had no idea how many of Christie's friends would be in the fort. Extra precautions had been taken to avoid publicizing the formation of this posse, and the party had quietly approached the area, under the cover of darkness. They could only hope that they had not been detected and Christie would not have time to muster his supporters. The attack on the fort was planned for daybreak, and for several hours after the meal Tolbert carefully went over his battle plan and each man's assignment. One group was selected to be the inner circle, and another group was chosen for the outer circle. The outer circle was to protect the party from any possible rear attack by Christie's friends, once the battle got underway.

At 4 A.M. the next morning, the posse moved out, each of its members thoroughly familiar with the battle plan and the position he was to take. Dave Rusk drove the wagon, and Tolbert, Ratterree, and White followed to the placement point they had selected for the cannon. The men unloaded the heavy gun near a large tree directly across the creek running in front of Christie's fort. The wagon had been driven along the creek bed, and the soft sand had enabled them to move into position quietly and undetected.

Once the cannon had been set and the barrel adjusted to fire directly into the cabin's front door, Tolbert surveyed the various positions and checked his watch. Presently a man emerged from the cabin. He was carrying a bucket and was apparently on his way to the nearby spring for water. At this point Christie's several dogs were awakened and began barking loudly. While Rusk and Tolbert aimed their rifles at the figure, Tolbert yelled out to him: "Throw up your hands. You're surrounded." The man leaped back into the cabin as Rusk's rifle ripped into the door.

For a brief moment there was complete silence while Tolbert waited for Christie's return fire. Soon Christie's barrage cut into the posse's tree cover from all sides of the fort. Tolbert gave the signal for return fire, and for several minutes the sounds of the raging battle, which could be heard as far away as Tahlequah, shattered the tranquility of the morning sunrise.

Tolbert signaled to cease fire and once more yelled out toward the cabin, "Christie, you are surrounded by federal lawmen. I'm giving you this one and only chance to surrender peaceably. We're prepared to stay this time until you're taken, and you have no means of escape." No answer came from the fort, and Tolbert yelled again, "If you have women and children in there, send them out now, and if you want to live, come out yourself and we will hold our fire." The front door slowly opened, and three Cherokee women and a small child ran toward them. Ben Knight asked one woman to tell them who was with Ned in the fort, but she refused to answer, and finally Tolbert sent her and the other two women and the child on their way.

It was learned sometime after the battle that Christie's companions were Arch Wolf, Bear Paw, and a young Cherokee boy named Charlie Soldierhair. Until recently, most writers and Christie historians were not aware of Bear Paw being in the fort since he escaped undetected in the final minutes of the battle. Cecil Atchison of Fort Smith, Arkansas, was given this information by Bear Paw's son, also called Bear Paw, a few years ago. The fact was not disclosed by the son until after his father's death because the family feared that court action would be taken against the elder Bear Paw and that he would probably be hanged on Parker's gallows.

Tolbert, still receiving no answer from Christie, then summoned their Cherokee guide, Ben Knight, to yell at Christie in Cherokee, carefully explaining that this time the lawmen were not going to leave until he was dead or captured. As expected, the only answer from the cabin was another heavy barrage of fire that sent the posse scurrying for cover on all sides of the fort.

As the battle continued well into midmorning, a sizable crowd of onlookers began to congregate near the site. Christie's father, Watt Christie, was among the onlookers, and Tolbert sent Ben Knight to ask Watt to help persuade his son to give up. Knowing his son would never surrender, however, Watt refused.

The battle continued for many hours, and the continuous rapid fire and accuracy of Christie and his companions kept the possemen pinned down. Tolbert had his men fashion some long sticks to which coal-oil-soaked rags were tied. The sticks were dropped down several rifle barrels and the rags ignited. The flaming arrows were then fired at the cabin repeatedly in an attempt to set it on fire. The meager fires were not sufficient to burn the heavy logs of the fort, however, and after several hours, this project was abandoned.

This left the posse with the cannon as the only means left for possibly destroying Christie's stronghold. After carefully preparing the cannon and resetting the barrel's aim, a proper measure of black powder was poured in, and the first projectile rammed in with a pole cut from a nearby tree. Tolbert ignited the fuse and sent forth the iron projectile in a belch of fire and black smoke. When the smoke cleared they noticed the projectile had cut deeply into the log but had relatively little effect on a wall that was two logs thick. All that afternoon the big gun was fired repeatedly into the cabin, and each firing drew a heavy barrage from the Indian for several minutes afterward. The large tree Tolbert and White used for cover while manning the big gun had been cut to shreds by the continuous fire from Christie's rifle.

After firing some thirty-seven rounds and doing little more damage to the fort than a few small holes in the roof, White and Tolbert decided to double the powder charge in one final attempt to blast out a wall of the fort. The mighty charge was too great for the small cannon, however, and the blast split the barrel, putting the cannon out of use. The sun was now beginning to set and Tolbert arranged for his tired possemen to go two at a time to camp for a short rest and a hearty meal that Becky had prepared. A full twelve hours of battle, some thirty-eight rounds from their cannon, and some two thousand rounds of rifle ammunition had brought them no closer to capturing Christie than when the battle had begun at dawn.

While the men took turns at eating, Tolbert, Rusk, White, and Charlie Copeland discussed their next approach. Copeland had been involved in the earlier attempt to capture Christie in which a burning wagon was used unsuccessfully. He noted that the remains of the wagon were nearby and the rear axle was still intact. Quietly securing the remaining wagon parts and some heavy oak planks from Christie's nearby sawmill, the men fashioned a rolling shield which they would use for a closer approach to the cabin.

Completing their rolling shield, they planned for Tolbert to guide the shield with the tongue that had been attached to the axle. Copeland was to approach the cabin behind the shield and, when close enough, run to the cabin wall and place six sticks of dynamite. Because of their ability at maintaining a barrage of rapid fire with rifles, Bill Smith and Bill

Ellis were selected to cover the men. Rusk also was placed at a strategic point to cover the approach.

Shortly after midnight Tolbert silently rolled the barricade across the clearing as Copeland, Ellis, and Smith crouched behind the oak plank shield. While Christie's fire was drawn a few yards from the fort, Smith and Ellis began their rapid fire, and Copeland ran to the wall. Placing the bundle of dynamite under the lower log the fuse was lit, and Copeland ran back to the shield. The barricade was pulled quickly back into the woods. Th enormous blast blew out an entire wall of the fort, and fire spread throughout the cabin from a stove overturned by the blast.

Gunfire continued throughout the night, and when dawn came flames had completely engulfed the cabin. Shooting ceased, and the possemen quietly held their positions, waiting for Christie to come out. Following a heavy cloud of black smoke pouring from the cabin, Christie suddenly leaped through the burning cabin wall and ran toward the possemen firing his two .44s and screaming the Cherokee death cry. He was so fast he ran right over Wess Bowman lying in the brush. Bowman then rolled over as he sent a bullet to Christie's temple killing him instantly. Sam Maples, who was crouching nearby, ran to Christie's body and emptied two revolvers into him, thus satisfying the burning revenge that had haunted him for four years.

Tolbert and the other possemen hurried to the scene. After identifying Christie's body they checked the burning structure and found only the young Cherokee boy, Charlie Soldierhair, in the cellar. He had been badly burned. While Christie had drawn the posse's attention by running out the front, Arch Wolf and Bear Paw had escaped undetected out the back of the fort. Christie was regarded as a hero by his followers for the courageous and suicidal action he took to cover his companion's successful escape.

After posing for several pictures by a photographer who had joined the group of spectators, the men collected their equipment and prepared to leave for Fayetteville, Arkansas, where a certificate of death would be issued for "the worst outlaw in the history of the Cherokee nation." From Fayetteville, the posse and Christie's body would return to Fort Smith by train.

The news of Christie's death and the return route by the heroic possemen spread rapidly, and large crowds gathered along the way to view the posse and the body of the man who had held off the United States' best lawmen for nearly five years. During the stopover at the Summers' store, Christie's body, which had been strapped to a plank from the door of his fort, was stood upright for pictures. Large crowds met the party at Fayetteville and Fort Smith. In Fort Smith the possemen were awarded many honors, and each was personally congratulated by Judge Isaac Parker while Christie's body was displayed on the steps of Parker's court. Deputy Marshal Hugh Harp placed his rifle in Christie's hands for one photo. Each of the deputies received a portion of the sizable reward money and also citations from Washington praising their heroic service. Watt Christie claimed his son's body a few days later and buried him in the secluded Christie cemetery near his home in what is now the community of Wauhillaw, Oklahoma.

A few months later Arch Wolf was captured by federal marshals in a Chicago hotel lobby. He was returned to Muskogee, Indian Territory, where he was tried in the district court that had been established there April 2, 1889. The records of this trial and sentence have been lost.

Young Sam Maples had thought of little else but killing Christie since the tragic day his father was killed in Tahlequah. Now that Christie was dead, Sam wanted to begin a new life and to try to forget his past. He left immediately after the battle for California and later went to Canada, where he spent the rest of his life and never returned to his native Bentonville.

Christie's death brought to an end many outlaw gangs'

activities in the area, and peace soon came to the border region. With this quieter environment, more and more white settlers moved into the Indian Territory. As the white population grew, so did the talk of statehood. Finally, in 1907, the proud Indian nation, which had struggled so long for their independence, became the state of Oklahoma.

Although Zeke Proctor and Ned Christie's struggles were some twenty years apart, their lives were comparable in many ways. In addition to their common abilities to sense danger, handle weapons, and their love of firewater, they succumbed to lives of crime by similar paths. Proctor's trouble began with an accidental shooting, and Christie was forced into a defensive position by a murder accusation of which he was cleared thirty years after his death. Both men were strong advocates of Cherokee national independence and the rights of the self-government their nation's treaties afforded them. Their resentment of federal involvement within their lands greatly contributed to their bitterness toward the government. Both held positions of leadership within the Cherokee nation's government. Proctor and Christie were accused of hundreds of crimes, yet neither was ever convicted of a crime of any kind in a court of law. During their lifetimes, both men attracted many friends and supporters to the cause for which they struggled. Proctor's followers grew to such numbers that the United States found it necessary to issue a treaty of pardon to prevent a major uprising. Realizing the hopelessness of this struggle, Proctor chose to accept this nation's only treaty with an individual. Christie also had many supporters, but as the years went by, his followers dwindled as his original purpose became secondary to his hatred and revenge. He had no choice of action other than death on Parker's gallows or by a marshal's gun. Succeeding in holding off America's best lawmen for nearly five years, he became the only known individual in history against which a cannon was used by lawmen.

The debates among frontier historians as to whether

Proctor and Christie should be remembered as desperate
outlaws, martyrs to the Cherokee cause, or simply victims of
a turbulent era in our country's history, will no doubt go on
indefinitely. It has not been the intent of this text to de-
termine the type of commemoration these men might de-
serve, but rather to examine the colorful lives of these, the
last of the Cherokee warriors, and their personal struggles
with the United States of America.

Ned Christie's tombstone in the Christie cemetery of Wauhillau, Oklahoma. The marker reads:

Born Dec. 14, 1852

Died Nov. 3, 1892

He was at one time a member of the Executive Council of the C. N. He was a black-smith and was a brave man.

Peek Above Wolf was with Ned Christie in his cabin during Christie's last fight. Wolf escaped through the rear of the cabin as Ned drew the marshals' fire by running out the front. Wolf was later cap-tured by U.S. marshals in a hotel lobby in Chicago. He was returned to Muscogee, Indian Territory, for trial in the federal court. This pic-ture was taken shortly after his capture. Note that his feet are chained. (Photo-graph courtesy Cecil Atchison Collection)

# BIBLIOGRAPHY

*BOOKS*

Cotterill, R. S. *The Southern Indians*. Norman: University of Oklahoma Press, 1954.

Foreman, Grant. *Indian Removal*. Norman: University of Oklahoma Press, 1966.

McKennon, C. W. *Iron Men*. New York: Doubleday & Company, 1967.

Shirley, Glenn. *Law West of Fort Smith*. Omaha: University of Nebraska Press, 1968.

Starr, Emmett. *History of The Cherokee Indians and Their Legends and Folklore*. Oklahoma City: The Warden Company, 1921.

Van Eaton, Frank L. *Hell on the Border*. n.p. n.d.

*NEWSPAPERS*

Adair County (Okla.) *Democrat-Gleaner*. Eli Whitmire account of Proctor trial, May 26, 1939.

Fort Smith (Ark.) *Southwest Times Record*. Sesquicentennial edition, Sunday, May 28, 1967.

Little Rock *Arkansas Gazette*. Indian Country editorial, May 10, 1872.

Newspaper articles owned by Beatrice Maples Jones about her grandfather. Fayetteville, Ark., and Bentonville papers, dates not recorded. These old newspaper clippings were originals from 1890's, and dates on papers were cut off at the time.

Oklahoma City *Daily Oklahoman*. "Tragedy of Going Snake Courthouse," by Grant Foreman, October 7, 1934.

Stillwell (Okla.) *Democrat-Journal*. Indian Country editorial, March 28, 1968.

Tulsa (Okla.) *Tulsa World*. Fred E. Sutton, editorial, 1922; Jake Alberty's Proctor Story, April, 1968; and "Life is Pleasant at Beckwith," 1969.

*PERIODICALS*

Brewington, E. H. "Cherokee," *Big West Magazine*, n.d.

Brown, Dee. "The Trail of Tears." *American History Illustrated,* VII (June, 1972), 30–39.
Dailey, Harry P. "Isaac Parker." *University of Arkansas Law School Bulletin,* XXVI (October 15, 1932).
Eubanks, R. Roger. "Christie's Story." *Sturm's Magazine* (June, 1910).
Meyers, Olevia. "Zeke Proctor—Outlaw or Lawman." *The West.* May, 1966.
*Scribners Magazine,* November, 1896.
Sturdevant, William C. "American Indian Religions." *American Way* (February, 1972).

### LETTERS

E. H. Brewington letters to A. D. Lester, Westville, Okla., 1968.
Congressman Ed Edmondson letter to A. D. Lester, Westville, Okla., 1967.
Dr. C. D. Gunter, Siloam Springs, Ark. letters to A. D. Lester, Westville, Okla., 1966.
Grant Foreman letters to Elizabeth Walden, Watts, Okla., regarding her grandfather Zeke Proctor, 1930, in Mrs Walden's possession.
U. S. Grant to 42nd Congress, May 10, 1872.
Dr. C. D. Gunter, Siloam Springs, Ark., letter to Phillip Steele, Springdale, Ark., 1970.
Dora Wolf letters to A. D. Lester, Westville, Okla., 1967.

### INTERVIEWS CONDUCTED BY A. D. LESTER

Various Cherokee citizens, Eastern Okla., 1935 to 1970.
Charlie Proctor, Proctor, Okla., 1950 to 1960
Zeke Proctor, Jr., Proctor, Okla., 1950 to 1960
Elizabeth Walden, Watts, Okla., 1950 to 1960
Moses Welch, Watts, Okla., 1937

### INTERVIEWS WITH PHILLIP STEELE

Cecil Atchison, Fort Smith, Ark., 1969 to 1970.
Dr. T. L. Ballenger, Tahlequah, Okla., 1970.
Kermit Beck, Flint, Okla., 1969 to 1970.
Bill Bolen, Marble City, Okla., 1969 to 1970.
Bill Chance, Chewey, Okla., 1969.
Bill Christie, Jr., Tahlequah, Okla., 1970.
Dr. C. D. Gunter, Siloam Springs, Ark., 1969.
A. D. Lester, Westville, Okla., 1969 to 1973.
Guy Nichols (historian), National Park Service, Fort Smith, Ark., 1969 to 1970.
Walter Proctor, Proctor, Okla., 1969.
Jim Reed, Fayetteville, Ark., 1969.
Nancy Runabout, Tahlequah, Okla., 1970.
Mitchell Sixkiller, Watts, Okla., 1970.
Elizabeth Walden, Watts, Okla., 1969 to 1970.

### GOVERNMENT DOCUMENTS

Acts of the Cherokee Council, 1872, Cherokee Historical Documents. Oklahoma Historical Society. Oklahoma City.
Census of the Cherokee Nation (1863, 1880, 1890, 1893, 1896). Oklahoma Historical Society. Oklahoma City.

Cherokee Court Records. Oklahoma Historical Society. Oklahoma City.

Cherokee Government Records. Oklahoma Historical Society. Oklahoma City.

Cherokee Headright Pay Records (payments authorized by the National Cherokee Council May 19, 1883). Oklahoma Historical Society, Oklahoma City.

Cherokee marriage laws, Oklahoma Historical Society, Oklahoma City.

Congressional Records 42nd Congress. Library of Congress. Washington, D.C.

Dawes Roll (1902). Oklahoma Historical Society. Oklahoma City.

Drennen Roll (1852). Oklahoma Historical Society. Oklahoma City.

Emigrant Roll (1835) National Archives. U.S. General Services Administration. Washington, D.C.

Federal court records (1850 to 1900), Federal Records Center. Fort Worth, Tex.

Going Snake District Roll (1880). Oklahoma Historical Society. Oklahoma City.

U. S. Grant letters to 42nd Congress. Library of Congress. Washington, D.C.

Letters and documents by Grant Foreman. Indian Archives, Oklahoma Historical Society. Oklahoma City.

Parker's court records. National Park Service, Parker's Court. Fort Smith, Ark.

U.S. Civil War Records. U.S. War Department, Records & Pension Office. Washington, D.C.

U.S. Department of Interior. Bureau of Pensions Records. Washington, D.C.

*UNPUBLISHED MATERIAL*

Atchison, Cecil. Indian and Arkansas border history collection, Fort Smith, Ark.

Brewington, E. H. The Beck mill. Oklahoma City.

Foreman, Grant. "The Tragedy at Going Snake Court House." Muskogee, Okla. Sent A. D. Lester some years ago; also appeared in Muskogee newspaper.

Gunter, Dr. C. D. Indian history collection. Siloam Springs, Ark.

Lester, A. D. Cherokee history collection. Westville, Okla.

———. Decendants of Ezekiel Proctor. Westville, Okla.

———. The Proctor Family, Westville, Okla.

Walden, Elizabeth. Her prize-winning story about Zeke Proctor, her grandfather, entered in the W.P.A. Pioneer History contest in 1930.

Cody Deering

*Cody*

3-4 great grandson